WITH GOD
ALL THINGS
ARE POSSIBLE!

Tim Clark

First published by Dog Ear Publishing
4010 W. 86th Street, Ste H
Indianapolis, IN 46268
www.dogearpublishing.net

ISBN: 978-145750-222-4

This book is printed on acid-free paper.

The views expressed in this material are my own and do not represent the views of any entity named in it.

Printed in the United States of America

TABLE OF CONTENTS

by Coach Doug Hayden

With God, All Things Are Possible is more than a book of Tim Clark's amazing life; it is the foundation of his positive attitude in the face of adversity. It has served as the motivation for his long list of amazing physical accomplishments despite his disabilities. It has shaped his perceptions of life and events in a culture that says "Look out for #1." It has kept him humble when he could easily gloat; it is what drives him forward when most of us would stand still. Why does it take someone with more challenges in life than most of us can understand to show us what is truly possible when we believe?

Tim weaves his own compelling and inspirational story with accounts of some of his favorite historical and cultural figures, as well as a few great sports stories that have shaped his life. He ties it all together with a call to trust and glorify God. As you journey through Tim's life from the day of his birth to today, you will get to know Tim, his admiration for his family, and his remarkable physical feats. You will also be challenged to do more with your own God-given talents.

I have only known Tim for a few of years, but as his swim coach, I was fortunate to play a small role in the event that, while only lasting 45 seconds, would become the catalyst for this book. We met very briefly at a company gathering of gold-medal winners for an event chronicled in this book called Kansas City Corporate Challenge (KCCC). Approximately fifteen of us were getting a picture taken for our company's quarterly publication. I didn't know many of the competitors since I was new to the company. I looked around and tried to figure out which sport each athlete had won. There were some young, very athletic-looking people, and a few middle-aged, former college athlete-types like myself.

I reached out my right hand to introduce myself to Tim. Without missing a beat, he grabbed my hand with his left, smiled and said, "Tim Clark, how ya doing?" I remember thinking, *Whoa, that guy is missing an arm*. It would not have surprised me in any other setting, but this was a group of KCCC gold medalists. The competition in the Corporate Challenge is stiff. There is no disabled category, and while everyone is encouraged to participate, you have to be pretty darn good to win a gold medal.

I found out Tim got first place in Doubles Table Tennis and began wondering, *How in the world does this guy even play table tennis? He only has one arm!* I had no idea at the time Tim was also born missing both legs at just about the knees.

The next week Tim and I rode together to the KCCC banquet. He had been nominated for the Alex George Award. This is a prestigious award given to one man and one woman out of 20,000+ athletes for outstanding sportsmanship. The more I learned about Tim, the more I felt he was the perfect example of everything the Alex George Award stood for. He had a long history of dominating his sport against ranked, able-bodied opponents despite his physical challenges. He exhibited humility and sportsmanship, and promoted the KCCC every chance he got. Although he didn't win the award that night, we hit it off right away. That night, we set off on a path that neither of us had imagined.

We worked in different buildings, so only saw each other occasionally. We had lunch a couple of times and kept in touch with email. Our main topic was always Corporate Challenge. A year and a half later, my job was reorganized into a different department, in a different building, and lo and behold, I was sitting about 20 feet from Tim's desk. Game on!

Tim and I talk a lot about coincidence, or more accurately, the lack of coincidence. We talk about the happenstance we perceive as coincidence being the hand of God gently touching our lives. He believes all things are of God, good or bad, success or failure, all the circumstances of his life have brought him to this God-given moment. Tim firmly believes that God shaped him in his mother's womb to go about doing good in this world. I've heard him say, "God could have made me anything he wanted to. He could have made me a rock, but, he didn't. He made me a guy with one arm and no legs. I'm blessed, and I feel it's my obligation to do the best I can with what God gave me to glorify his name."

Maybe being thankful for what we have, instead of wanting what we don't, is why it takes someone like Tim to show us what is possible when we believe.

With all he has accomplished, I believe Tim is just beginning his journey. As Tim's story unfolds, you'll be amazed at his tenacity, dedication, and perseverance.

It's Not Bout You

I t was finally time for my swim heat. It was the Kansas City Corporate Challenge Swim Meet. My date with destiny had arrived.

Christine told me to get into the water. "DST! DST! DST!" Christine shouted.

"Come on, Tim!" somebody yelled from the crowd. All the preparation and training were about to pay off.

A few minutes earlier, Doug, my swimming coach, had given me his last piece of advice: "Relax on the first twenty-five, get traction in the water, and then bring it home!"

"Swimmers, on your mark." Beep!

The date was February 24, 1968, and our family doctor, Charles Zammar, had just come in from the delivery room at Conley Maternity Hospital in Kansas City, Missouri, with me in his arms and a bit of a stressed look on his face. "Well, Mr. Clark, there are, unfortunately, some abnormalities. Your son is missing his right arm below the elbow and both legs below the knees." Dr. Zammar explained. Ultrasound technology was in its infancy back then, so my parents had had no warning of the surprise that awaited them at the hospital on my birthday. My parents had gone to the delivery room that day with all the hopes and dreams that await all new parents. The possibilities could be endless. Would their newborn baby grow up to be a doctor, a lawyer, a senator, or maybe a professional athlete? Most important of all, would he be healthy?

My parents already had three other children. They had two sons, Dan and Cam, who were six and eight, respectively. They also had a two-year-old daughter named Rhonda. I would be the fourth and, as it turned out, the last. Many people would have expected my parents to be devastated by the news of my deformities, but my parents were amazingly calm instead. To this day, my dad remembers that I looked right in his eyes and he just said, "It's God's will." My mom would later say the same thing. The one thing that God knew I would need from the very beginning was great parents. He knew that I would need unselfish parents, and that is exactly what he gave me. My parents handled the new set of cards they had been dealt like champions. Challenges lay ahead, but my parents had clearly passed the initial test.

Some people believe that we live in a world where events are just random and there's really no rhyme or reason for anything. I, on the other hand, believe in a sovereign God who oversees every minute little detail of the universe and of our individual lives. Psalm 139:13-16 says, "For You created my inmost being; You knit me together in my mother's womb. I praise You because I am fearfully and wonderfully made; Your works are wonderful, I know that full well. My frame was not hidden from You when I was made in the secret place. When I was woven together in the depths of the earth, your eyes saw my unformed body. All the days ordained for me were written in Your book before one of them came to be."

A nurse at Conley Maternity Hospital was really encouraging and was a big influence on my mother. She told my mom in no uncertain terms, "Don't let anyone ever pity him." She also told her, "When he acts up, you treat him just like all of your other kids. Don't treat him any differently." My mom took that advice to heart. I know, as I remember getting some very unwanted spankings growing up. I'm sure I deserved a few more. My parents raised me just like they had raised all their other three children. I don't remember feeling like I was any different. Unfortunately, my brothers and sister didn't treat me any differently, either, and picked on me just like they would any younger brother.

Dr. Zammar spent some time showing my parents some of the latest artificial limb technologies that were available and what could be coming in the near future. He showed them that with prosthetic limbs, people could go on to live relatively normal, productive lives, so amidst all the new fears and uncertainties my parents had to be facing, there were many voices of hope as well. It's as if God was whispering into my parents' ears, "It's going to be all right. I have a plan."

Several weeks went by after my eventful birthday; my parents were back home, trying to figure out how to conquer all the new challenges we were going to face. My dad went back to work at AT&T, where he had been employed for more than ten years. My mom went back to her decorative painting class that she attended weekly. One week, my mom and the decorative painting teacher started talking about some of the special needs I had; it was a conversation that would bless us for years to come. Her teacher's name was Gini Antoine, and after hearing about my situation, Gini knew exactly where I needed to be. She referred my mother to a local Shriner by the name of Floyd Carson. Gini believed that Floyd could possibly sponsor me and get me admitted to Shriners Hospital in St. Louis, Missouri.

Floyd Carson owned Carson's Funeral Home in Independence, Missouri, and after a phone call from my mother, he came over to the house and met my parents and me. Shriners Hospital for Crippled Children provided medical care and services for crippled children at no cost to the parents. This would be critical for our situation because I would need new prosthetic legs made every year or two until I was 18 years of age. Floyd Carson turned out to be a blessing from God and sponsored me to be admitted into the hospital.

Before I could be fitted for prosthetic legs, however, I needed to have two surgeries, one on each leg. For the first two years of my life, I spent quite a bit of time in and out of Shriners Hospital in St. Louis. After recovering from the surgeries, I was fitted for my prosthetic legs and began the long road of trying to learn how to walk on them.

I've heard many of the horror stories about Ann Kelly and myself. She was the physical therapist unfortunate enough to have the impossible task of trying to teach stubborn, hardheaded, little ole me how to walk. She told my parents on several occasions that she had gone home with a splitting headache because of me. She said it in love, of course.

It wasn't until my parents would take me on vacation in Minnesota that I would finally take my first steps without holding on, right out of my parent's arms. My athletic career had begun.

My prosthetist at Shriners Hospital was Mr. Leo Tippy. Mr. Tippy, as we called him, was a very funny and likeable guy. He always made what would normally be a rather undesirable process of being fitted for prosthetic limbs at least tolerable. Mr. Tippy and I became pretty good friends over the first 18 years of my life because every year or two I needed to be measured for new prosthetic limbs. Mr. Tippy had the incredible ability of being able to read my mind and figure out exactly what was bothering me or didn't fit just right. That's a very important talent to have for someone who makes limbs for kids, because kids can't always communicate what hurts and where. One thing is for certain: I could not have handpicked anyone better to have made my legs for me. Mr. Tippy was the best.

Prosthetic legs have been a tremendous blessing over the course of my life. I can't even imagine my life without them. The technology has improved every year and allowed people missing legs to live very normal lives. I didn't feel that way about the artificial arm they tried to make me wear, however. I remember hating it from the very beginning. The people at Shriners Hospital thought the arm would help me one day, but I wanted no part of it. The straps were very uncomfortable, and I sweated horribly when I had it on. The worst part was that the arm had an ugly metal hook on the end of it that would hit me in the eye from time to time. You've only got to give yourself a couple of black eyes before artificial arms are off your Christmas list.

My life from the beginning had its share of difficulties and challenges, but from a very early age, I always believed that God had a purpose for me being born the way I was and that purpose wasn't about me, it was about God. In John 9:2-3, the disciples ask Jesus, "Who sinned, this man or his parents, that he was born blind?" Jesus answered them, "Neither this man nor his parents sinned, but this happened so that the work of God might be displayed in his life." God has a purpose for all of our lives. God's purpose may not line up with our desires, our wants, our ambitions, and our goals, but it's not about us. Life is about God.

My early years at home were pretty typical. There were plenty of football and baseball games played on the living and family room floors when my parents were away. I also recall a few unexpected trips to the emergency room. On one occasion, at the age of three, I ran away from a humongous black spider in my bedroom only to fall backward off the bed and break my collarbone. That spider didn't know how lucky he was. Another time, I tripped over my own two prosthetic feet and hit my head on the gas can in the garage. That opened up a gash that took two big stitches to close. Overall, however, I remember a very happy childhood with plenty of love, support, and adventure. Every summer, all went as a family on vacation to Park Rapids, Minnesota. My great aunt Violet and great uncle Warren had a wonderful home right on Potato Lake in northern Minnesota. Right beside their home, they had built a guesthouse so family and friends could visit them throughout the year. It not only provided our family an affordable vacation every year but also created some of the best memories of our lives. I'm sure my dad might disagree, but some of the most fun times were during the 14-hour trips in the station wagon from Independence, Missouri, to Park Rapids, Minnesota. Every couple of hours, my brothers, sister and I would take turns asking the universal kid vacation question, "Are we there yet?" Of course the answer was always the same: "Not yet."

As I approached the age of five, my parents had to start making some decisions on where I would go to school. A nurse at Shriners Hospital encouraged them not to put me in a school for crippled children because she didn't think I would get the quality of education that I needed to succeed, so my parents decided that I would start out in the public school system. William Southern Elementary School was right at a mile from where we lived. I would end up spending the first seven years of my academic journey there. In preparation for my first day of kindergarten, I remember, my mom got all of my pants fixed up with hooks so I could easily button my pants with one hand. If necessary, I would just ask my teacher to tie my shoes. Other than that, I was raring to go. I was going to be a bulldog.

My kindergarten teacher was Jana Cummings. Mrs. Cummings was friendly and very pretty, too. She helped me out a lot in my first year in the public school system. I think she was a little concerned at first whether or not she would be able to handle a special situation like mine.   As time went on, though, she would communicate to my parents that it was working out just fine. She said that if any-thing, the problem was that I didn't ask for enough help. She would end up being a big influence on my parents deciding to keep me in the public schools for years to come.

My first-grade teacher at William Southern was Rosemary Meyers. She was really nice. She would teach me to read some of my very first words. I also recall that it was in first grade that my desire for competition began. I remember watching the other kids play kickball and other games at school.   I wanted badly to get out there and participate. I have had a love and passion for sports my whole life and have always been extremely competitive. I know that God placed those desires and passions inside of me too. Your passions and talents should guide you to your destiny.

When I was eight, my mom signed me up for some bowling lessons at the local bowling alley, Strike 'N Spare. I wasn't very good, but I sure enjoyed it. I was happy because at least I was in the game. The problem I had in bowling was that with prosthetic legs, I would be off-balance half the time when I released the ball. I would get a spare and then turn right around and throw a gutter ball. That wasn't good. Late in the bowling season, I started to get a really sharp pain in the bottom part of my left leg. When I went to the doctor, it was determined that I had a bone spur in my left leg. If left untreated, my bone would keep growing until it broke completely through the skin. Surgery was going to be needed to cut the bone back down in size. By this time, I was in second grade and would have to take a month or two off from school to go back to Shriners Hospital for surgery. I wasn't too happy about the whole thing.

The only part of our four-and-a-half-hour car trips to St. Louis that I always enjoyed was seeing the Gateway Arch, the gateway to the west. My parents and I went up to the top of it a couple of times. It was pretty cool and had quite a view from the top. For the biggest parts of our trips, however, I would normally just be curled up in the back seat sleeping. If and when I ever did wake up, I would usually talk to my parents or play little games like trying to get truckers to honk their horns or wave. They would usually comply.

On the trips to St. Louis, my dad would always drive. Dad always seemed like he enjoyed driving but I also think he just knew it was his responsibility. My mom would keep him company and keep him awake by talking to him about all kinds of things. The trip to the hospital to have my bone spur removed would be different in only one major way: I wouldn't be making the trip back home, at least not for about a month.

I remember being quite scared going into the surgery. I wasn't allowed to have any food or drink the night before because my surgery was scheduled for 8:00 a.m. All I recall from surgery day was that they gave me a shot and then I became really sleepy. Then they wheeled me into a high-tech room with extremely bright lights and asked me to move onto a cold black table. The next thing I knew, I woke up in the recovery room with a severe pain in my left leg. I remember the strangest part was how quickly time had gone by when they put me under. It felt like only ten minutes had passed, but it had actually been ten hours. In any case, the scariest and worst part was behind me, at least as far as the surgery was concerned.

I had a big cast on my left leg after the surgery. Of course my leg would itch everywhere I couldn't scratch. The cast also came up so high on my leg that I couldn't bend my knee. To say the least, I couldn't wait to get that darn cast off. They told me I would have to have the cast on for only about three weeks. It seemed like three years to me.

Not having my parents there was the worst part. They made the trip back to St. Louis every weekend to visit me, but visiting hours were only three hours on the weekends so when my parents would first arrive, I would constantly watch the clock, counting down the three hours until the time they would have to leave. I was sure happy to see them, though. My mom would bring me all the cards from my William Southern classmates, teacher, and principal. Every day or two, they were all kind enough to send me a

get-well card telling me how much they missed me
and were looking forward to my return. It all made
me anxious to get well and get back home.

Three weeks passed, and I was excited and ready
to get my cast off. I had come up with every creative
way I could think of to stick various objects down my
cast to scratch my leg. I remember that the experience of getting the cast removed was terrifying. Seeing and hearing the power saw a couple of inches
from my leg was enough to send me over the edge. It
would probably be enough to send almost any eight-
year-old over the edge. For some reason, the words
"Don't worry, we won't cut you" didn't seem to calm
my nerves. I was scared to death. A short twenty
minutes later, however, they were done and I could
see my leg again. I don't think my leg ever looked so
beautiful to me. The strangest part was that it would
take several weeks before I would be able to bend my
leg again at the knee.

About a month after my surgery, my parents were
back to pick me up and take me home. Luckily for
me, they hadn't decided to use my surgery as an
opportunity to finally get rid of me. My parents had
actually planned several things for us to do in St.
Louis before returning home, but I was homesick and
just wanted to head straight home and get ready to go
back to school.

On my first day back to school, I received a hero's
welcome from my classmates and friends. I was
amazed at how much they seemed to have missed me.
When I came back I had to get around in a wheelchair
for about a month. My mom took me to school every

day. Getting that wheelchair in and out of the car was quite the challenge. Just ask her. Wheelchair or not, I was just happy that my world was getting back to normal. My second-grade teacher, Ms. Hansen, was very gracious in helping me get all caught up on my schoolwork.

After a few weeks had passed, I was finally able to get my left prosthetic leg on and go back to school without a wheelchair. That certainly made my mom a lot happier. It's amazing how much someone can appreciate having prosthetic legs after having to live two months without them. Just being able to walk around with my friends and to feel normal again was a great feeling.

After getting home from school everyday I usually just sat down at the kitchen table and did a little homework. Then I would go out in the backyard and play with our neighborhood friendly dog, Shaggy. That's what I named him, anyway. He belonged to the people who lived behind us. They didn't take very good care of him and let him just roam around wherever he wanted. Shaggy and I became like best friends. Whenever it was cold in the winter, I would just open the garage door and let Shaggy come in and warm up. I would sit downstairs in the garage, petting Shaggy for hours. My mom would always buy dog food for me to give to him. That dog was practically a member of our family.

Growing up with two brothers and a sister played a major role in shaping me into the person I am today. Having to learn to share with three other siblings is a practical way for God to teach us that life is not all about us. All four of us spent a lot of time together as a family and created some unforgettable moments. Outside of having to referee a few senseless arguments and breakup a couple of all out brawls, Mom and Dad had a fairly easy time raising us four upstanding citizens. They might have a different opinion about how easy it was though.

My oldest brother, Cam, was a good athlete growing up and was really competitive too. I can't help but think that some of his competitive nature probably rubbed off on me too. He was eight years older than I was, so it would be quite a few years before I could be much competition for him. Cam was an excellent soccer player and very good at baseball too. We would on many occasions get together with all the neighborhood kids and play some memorable two-handed touch-football games. I always liked being on Cam's team because we would usually win. I remember going to watch many of Cam's baseball games when I was growing up. Cam always played exceptionally hard. I always knew that Cam may not steal every base or catch every fly ball, but at the end of the game, his uniform would be filthy and his elbows would be bloody. Growing up watching that had an impact on me.

Unfortunately, one of Cam's baseball games that my mom, sister, and I went to was nearly a disaster. I was nine years old at the time, and my dad was out of town on a business trip. Cam was at the plate when he fouled a pitch off to the side where we were sitting. My sister and I saw the ball and ran up to the fence to get away from it. My mom, however, did not see the ball and looked up just in time to catch it with her nose. It was the most horrible, scary sound I could imagine. Blood was immediately everywhere. Mom's nose was broken instantly. They told her later at the hospital that if the ball had hit her half an inch higher, it could have killed her. Thank God for His amazing grace.

My other brother, Dan, was six years older than I was. He wasn't interested in sports like Cam and I were growing up. Dan was more creative and smart. He was more of the practical thinker and brains in the family. Whenever I would get any presents for Christmas that needed assembling, I would always turn to Dan to help me put them together.

On more than one occasion, Dan's quick thinking skills helped us four kids escape big trouble from our parents. One time when my parents were away, we had one of our traditional family-room football games. As most of you are probably aware, it's not a real party until something gets broken. I recall dropping back to pass only to overthrow my brother Cam by a couple of long yards, knocking my mom's favorite eagle lamp off the table. To everyone's horror, one of the eagle's wings broke off, sending all four of us into a major panic attack. Dan was our only hope to escape Mom's wrath. It was in moments like these that I learned the importance of prayer. I vowed that I would go to church twice a week for the rest of my life if that eagle would miraculously sprout some new wings before my parents got home.

God must have heard my pathetic call for help, as Dan's emergency repair skills proved effective enough to keep Mom from finding out. It would be years later before the four of us kids would muster up enough courage to confess our crime.

There were other times when we needed to call on Dan to come to the rescue. I remember going through a phase in my youth when I would capture various insects and keep them sort of as pets in an aquarium in my room. My two favorite insects were caterpillars and praying mantises. I liked watching caterpillars spin their cocoons and then become moths or butterflies. Praying mantises fascinated me by the way they went about killing their prey. Both caterpillars and praying mantises are a couple of God's awesome little creatures. I'll never forget the time my caterpillar Fuzzy Tiger climbed out of my aquarium and hid itself somewhere in my bedroom. My mom, sister, and I looked for hours, trying to find that little caterpillar. Finally, we decided to give up and wait for Dan to come home and help us out. When Dan arrived, he came into my bedroom and asked himself this question out loud: "If I were a caterpillar, where would I go?" Then he answered his own question: "I would go to something green." Then Dan walked right over to my green blanket that was at the end of my bed and turned it over. I could not believe my eyes. That darn caterpillar was sitting right there. We inducted Dan into the emergency rescue team hall of fame that night.

It's kind of ironic that even though Dan was not really into sports growing up, he would be the one to play perhaps the most critical role in my athletic future. During the summer breaks, we would go over to Aunt Sue's apartment pool to swim and play with our cousins. Over the course of a couple of months, Dan taught me how to swim. The key to swimming for me was simply getting over my fear of the water. One thing that helped me in the water was that I was very buoyant. Dan simply took me under the water multiple times and let go of me. Then when I would start to get in any kind of trouble, he would grab me and start all over again. He just repeated that process until my fear of the water was gone and I was able to swim on my own. Swimming came very naturally to me. It would be years down the road before I would fully realize this gift God had given me.

One of the funniest memories I have from growing up with Dan was when we went out on Halloween dressed up as a two-headed monster. Dan carried me on his shoulders for miles that night, trick-or-treating for candy from door to door. We received some crazy reactions from neighbors opening their doors that night. I probably had more fun than Dan did, but it was clearly a night to remember. We definitely would have won any creative costume award that year.

My sister, Rhonda, was just a couple of years older than I was. She deserves a lot of credit for just surviving growing up with three brothers like us. Rhonda was a good athlete too. She was good at basketball and softball. The sport that she excelled at most, however, was bowling. I never wanted to go bowling with Rhonda because I had no chance at winning. Who wants to get beat badly by their sister? Rhonda and I shared a bedroom for a few years until we had the basement finished in our house. Rhonda and I were fairly close as far as brothers and sisters go. Of course we had our share of silly little fights over the years, but overall, we got along pretty well. I remember Rhonda being a real source of encouragement to me when I faced challenges at school and in life in general. She could always see the positive side of any situation. We all need someone like that in life.

Every once in a while I believe God can allow a natural disaster or two just to remind everyone that life is not all about us. Thunderstorms and tornadoes always seem to put the fear of God in my heart too: maybe that's by design. When I was nine years old, a once-in-a-five-hundred-year rainstorm came though Independence, Missouri. It rained 16 inches in less than 24 hours. At that time, the drainage system around our neighborhood was not very good, and whenever it rained a great deal over a short time, water would rise around our street corner. Normally, the water would rise to a certain level and then begin to recede and not cause any flooding in our house. This storm, however, was worse than any storm we'd ever seen. I remember thinking when the rain was pouring down that this must have been like it was back in the days of Noah in the Bible. That night was absolute chaos at our house. We felt pretty hopeless, seeing the water begin to rise to a dangerous level and knowing we could do nothing about it. We knew it wasn't a matter of if our basement was going to flood, but of by how many feet of water it would be flooded. All six of us were frantically bringing things upstairs from the basement so they wouldn't get wet.

It had been only a few years since my parents had finished the basement and built two bedrooms down there for Dan and Cam to live in. The water coming into the basement was nasty sewage water. It didn't smell very good. Everything was put in perspective for us, however, when we saw one man who had foolishly climbed out of his floating car, holding onto a street sign pole for dear life. The fire department ultimately rescued that man from certain drowning from the floodwaters. By the end of the night, we had two feet of water in our basement. The good news was that nobody was hurt or seriously injured. We had just lost some material possessions and received a great deal of flood damage to our basement. After several months of hard work, life went on and eventually went back to normal. God would help us get through it.

Back in school, my competitive nature started to come out in various arenas. As early as the third and fourth grades, I recall being extremely competitive with math races that the teachers would hold at the chalkboard. Math was always one of my best subjects, and I enjoyed racing, especially winning.

My first taste of any real success came a couple of years later when I won the William Southern Elementary School spelling bee in sixth grade. I even remember the word that I won with: raisin. It's amazing the little things that stick in our minds from youth. I spent the next couple of months after the spelling bee preparing for the district spelling bee, which would be held at Truman High School. I had been given a very large book of potential words to study. My mom went over thousands of words with me, trying to get me ready. When the event day arrived, I suffered from a huge case of stage fright and was out on the first word. I can't even remember what the word was. I was honestly just relieved that it was over.

Later that same year, I got my first taste of athletic success when I won the basketball free throw-shooting contest at William Southern Elementary School. That was quite a thrill for me. My physical education teacher, Mrs. Potts, was really happy for me. Over the next several weeks, she came early every morning to the school to open the gym for me to practice. I spent long hours shooting hundreds of free throws in the gym. To everyone's amazement, I went on to the district competition at Blue Springs, Missouri, and won again, making 17 out of 25 free throws. At that point, I felt like a hero in the eyes of my school and classmates. I had never had so much attention. My big run would come to an end the week after the district competition in Warrensburg, Missouri, at the state tournament. By that time, however, my love for competitive sports and the thrill of victory had taken root. I was hooked.

In sixth grade, many of my friends and classmates started playing musical instruments. With only one hand, I narrowed my choice of instruments to the French horn and the trumpet. The trumpet sounded better and looked cool to me. Those factors were enough to persuade me to start playing the trumpet. My dad's cousin Richard Smith had played trumpet with the Kansas City Philharmonic for several years. We approached Richard to see what type of instrument I should purchase. Our timing could not have been more perfect, because he had a trumpet that he was no longer using and was looking to sell. It was a beautiful silver Bach Stradivarius trumpet in great condition. That brand was like the Rolls Royce of trumpets at the time. He sold it to us for the bargain price of $200.00. I was so excited. Over the next three years, I dove head first into the trumpet playing. I became as competitive about playing the trumpet as about any sport I would ever take up. I played in music class in sixth grade and also took private lessons twice per week. I enjoyed the challenge of trying to improve my skills and hit higher notes. Over the following two years, I became the first chair in the trumpet section, proving that hard work really does pay off.

As I approached the end of my sixth-grade year at William Southern Elementary School, my parents and I sat down to talk about where I might go to junior high school for seventh and eighth grades. The principal at William Southern, Mr. Craven, and my P.E. teacher, Mrs. Potts, both thought it would be best for me to attend Bridger Junior High School because it had an elevator. That would make it much easier for me to travel between floors and access all of my classes. They feared that I might fall or get knocked down the stairs if I were to attend Palmer Junior High School. I wasn't really worried about falling down any stairs. I just wanted to go to school at Palmer because that was where most of my good friends were going. My parents wanted me to go wherever I would be the happiest, so after a couple of months of contemplation, the final decision was rendered. I decided to follow my heart and my friends to Palmer Junior High School. It was off to seventh grade and becoming a teenager. I was growing up.

The biggest immediate difference I noticed between junior high school and elementary school was the number of fights that took place. I don't know what it is about boys turning 13, but they seemed to be a lot more aggressive. I remember the gym teacher at Palmer breaking up fights almost every day. The gym teacher would give the rest of us a great incentive not to fight, however: on more than one occasion, I saw him hand out some painful-looking swats with a large board. I knew I wanted no part of that. I just did my best to focus on my classes and mind my own business.

When I became a teenager, girls became an object of interest as well. My biggest problem with girls was that I only liked the really pretty ones. For one reason or another, though, the really pretty ones didn't seem to be too interested in me. They always seemed to like the football players and athletic types. I guess they just couldn't see my future potential. Anyway, it just made it that much easier for me to focus on my schoolwork and on playing the trumpet. For the next two years, my life would consist of studying textbooks and taking music lessons.

My band instructor in junior high school was Mr. Elton. He made music a lot of fun because he was a very likeable and good-natured guy. Everyone liked him. He was kind and very accommodative in his handling of my special situation. Whenever we approached marching band performances, he asked me what I was capable of and what I felt comfortable doing. Mr. Elton was also quick thinking and gracious at getting me through a few awkward situations. One time, several of us students were all sitting around on a table, talking to Mr. Elton at the end of music class. I was sitting on the table with my leg hanging over the edge, swinging it back and forth. I watched in horror as my left leg fell off onto the ground without notice. It was one of those moments in life when I wanted to run into the closet and come out on another planet. Mr. Elton simply picked my leg up, made a really quick joke that had everyone laughing, and rescued me from what could have been an extremely embarrassing moment. To be truthful, because of the cool way Mr. Elton handled the whole situation, I felt like everyone seemed to admire and respect me more after that. Mr. Elton was a great guy and teacher.

In seventh grade, I held the first chair trumpet spot the whole year pretty much unchallenged. It wasn't until eighth grade that another young, talented, hungry trumpet player gave me all the competition I could handle. I held him off until the final month of my eight-grade year. I practiced for the competition as hard as I could and had no regrets. I had been first chair for almost two straight years. He just flat-out beat me. I played my best, but he was better.

I was a pretty skinny teenager. I wouldn't bulk up until I started lifting weights in high school. In junior high school, I was very competitive about getting good grades. I was almost obsessed with getting a perfect report card. In my two years at Palmer, I received only one B on my report card. The rest of my grades were all A's. It's kind of funny that my one B came in none other than my special P.E. class. That teacher made me so mad back then; I felt like she just had to prove to everyone what a tough teacher she was. I didn't think she would have given me an A no matter what I did. I'm sure I was a little biased. Despite my disappointment, however, I would make the National Honor Society in each of my seventh- and eighth-grade years. I don't believe that I was all that intelligent. As I look back, I just think that when I have set my mind to achieving a goal in life, more often than not, I have been successful. There's definitely something to be said about the human spirit and will.

In Luke 12:16-21, Jesus told the crowd a parable: "The ground of a certain rich man produced a good crop. He thought to himself, 'What shall I do? I have no place to store my crops.' Then he said, 'This is what I'll do. I will tear down my barns and build bigger ones, and there I will store all my grain and my goods. And I'll say to myself, "You have plenty of good things laid up for many years. Take life easy; eat, drink and be merry."' But God said to Him, 'You fool! This very night your life will be demanded from you. Then who will get what you have prepared for yourself?' This is how it will be with anyone who stores up things for himself, but is not rich toward

God." Some have interpreted this story to say that God is opposed to the accumulation of money. I don't believe the problem with the rich man in the parable was that he had a lot of money. Contrary to what many think, God is not opposed to wealth or people having a lot of it. In fact, Deuteronomy 8:18 says, "But remember the Lord your God, for it is He who gives you the ability to produce wealth." I believe God called the rich man a fool because he thought life was all about him. He thought he was the one who made the sun rise and the sun set. He thought he gave himself all of his talents. God wasn't even on the rich man's radar screen. For many, the most difficult lesson to learn in life is that it's not about them. It never has been, and it never will be. It's about God. We were all made by God and for God. Until we begin to see that, life won't make any sense and can seem incredibly unfair. To put it another way, God was trying to tell this rich man, "You fool! It's not about you!"

CHAPTER 2

Don't Be A Tiger. Just Be You!

Growing up, one of my favorite athletes to watch was Kansas City's very own professional golfer Tom Watson. I will never forget Watson's miracle chip on the 17th green that went straight into the hole to win the 1982 U.S. Open Championship. That was an incredible shot! On Saturdays or Sundays, I always checked the leader board to see how Watson was doing. I especially loved to watch when Tom Watson and Jack Nicklaus were battling it out for first. They were two great players whom everyone looked up to and wanted to emulate. As Watson and Nicklaus' careers started winding down, golf lost a lot of its excitement and appeal to me. That was until the mid to late '90s, when a young man by the name of Tiger Woods came on the scene. Tiger Woods brought the game of golf back to life as far as I was concerned. He brought athleticism to the game that had never been seen before. Tiger not only was awesome to watch but forced everyone else to either get better or get left behind. Tiger Woods did for the game of golf what Magic Johnson, Larry Bird, and Michael Jordan had

Tim Clark

for basketball: He took the game of golf to a whole new level.

Starting in the late 1990s, much of what we heard whenever we turned on our televisions was "Be a Tiger", which would be great advice if that were even remotely possible. I remember looking down at my one-armed, no-legged frame, wondering how anyone could even suggest something so ridiculous. I can't be Tiger Woods. I wish I could be. I think he's great. The only problem is that he has unique talents and gifts that God gave only to Tiger Woods. I could practice golf 24 hours a day, 7 days a week, for the next ten years and would not be anywhere close to being Tiger Woods. You know what, though? Tiger Woods can't be me, either. Not that he would want to be, but God has given me unique talents and gifts that He has not given to anyone else. What you have to do is find out where God has gifted you and pursue it with everything you've got. Don't waste your time and efforts in life trying to be someone else. Just be you!

In the fall of 1982, I began my freshman year at Truman High School in Independence, Missouri. We were the first freshman class ever to enter Truman High School. In the past, ninth graders had gone to school at the junior high schools in their districts. I spent the next four years at Truman following in the footsteps of my older brother Dan, and my older sister, Rhonda. Rhonda and I would spend the next two years going to school together at Truman High School. We would run into each other from time to time in the hallways between classes and occasionally in the lunchroom. It helped having an older sister ahead of me to give me some guidance on which classes to take and which teachers to avoid.

One of the first things I remember about entering high school was trying out for the Truman High School band. I had just spent the past two years at Palmer Junior High as the first- or second-chair trumpet player in the band and had no idea how I might do at the high school level. There were 15 trumpet positions open in the band at Truman, and I thought it was likely I could fill one of them. Gary Love was the band teacher at the school and was a little bit intimidating when it came time to go before him and tryout. I can recall being all nervous and scared and not believing that I had done very well when I went home. Mr. Love must have heard something different, though, because he ended up giving me the sixth chair out of 15 in the band. Sixth out of 15 as a freshman was way beyond my expectations and was higher than any other freshman. I was extremely pleased with the results and excited about starting my high school career on such a high note.

Playing in the high school band was really fun during football season. I felt like our music was relevant when we were playing for the crowd and trying to inspire our home football team on to victory. Deep down in my heart, though, I wanted to be out on the field, throwing a game-winning touchdown pass late in the fourth quarter. From the time I was a little kid, I have dreamed about being a great athlete.

I enjoyed music for a while, but it never quite quenched my soul's thirst for victory. After my sophomore year, I quit playing the trumpet and then completely focused on getting my body in shape for sports. I was destined to be an athlete.

I started working out with weights regularly at the beginning of my freshman year in high school. When I started lifting, I could only bench forty lbs with my left arm. By my senior year, I could bench nearly three times that amount. I became pretty radical about working out and eating right. I can remember eating nothing but tuna fish, eggs, and protein shakes for literally months, trying to get stronger. I felt guilty if I ate a candy bar or anything unhealthy during the radical fitness trip I was on. I was in the best shape of my life, though, and was just waiting for the right sport and opportunity to come along.

Six months from my 17th birthday, all of my friends were already driving and showing off their cool cars to each other. I wanted to learn how to drive and get my driver's license. Like always, my parents were supportive and thought I should go through the driver's education classes provided by the Rehabilitation Institute of Kansas City, whose mission is to help children and adults with disabilities become independent and productive members of society.

The first thing the Rehabilitation Institute did was to put me through an evaluation process to determine what adaptations would need to be done to a vehicle for me to be able to drive safely. They had me sit down into a driving simulator where I watched a video and pretended like I was driving a real car. After a couple of weeks, they determined that I would need only a spin knob put on the steering wheel and a plastic pedal extension added so I could use my left leg for the gas and the brake. I had a lot more control with my left leg because it extends just past the knee. My right leg ends right at the knee, giving me little or no control for pressing on the gas or brake pedals.

My parents then had the two accommodations recommended by the Rehabilitation Institute made to their 1983 Pontiac Grand Prix so I could begin the driver's education classes. Getting behind the wheel of a car is terrifying when you're first starting out. I'm sure that missing three limbs added a little bit of excitement for not only me but my driver's education instructor as well. I definitely wanted to make sure that my left prosthetic leg hit the brake and not the gas pedal. That would not be good. To be completely honest, though, driving a car always came pretty easy to me. The analysis they had done for what accommodations I would need was sound, and made the process of me learning how to drive and operate a vehicle relatively smooth. The only thing I can recall that gave me a lot of trouble was parallel parking. I think I flunked that test every single time.

The Rehabilitation Institute did an excellent job of training me to drive. I passed both the written and driving tests the very first times that I took them. I do remember failing parallel parking again, however. I'm not sure I could parallel park to this day. I always do my best to avoid it.

My parents spoiled me and gave me the 1983 Grand Prix to drive. They said it would be my graduation present. That was quite a graduation present and one sweet car. I was driving to Truman High School everyday in style!

I grew up a huge Kansas City Royals fan. My dad and I listened to nearly every game from the mid 1970s through the 1980s. Some of my favorite players were George Brett, Willie Wilson, Frank White, Hal McRae, Amos Otis, and Dan Quisenberry. Those were the glory days of Royals baseball. I really loved listening on the radio to play-by-play announcers Denny Mathews and Fred White. They made nearly every game exciting to listen to. As Royals fans, we had to live through some heartbreaking losses when the Royals lost to the Yankees in the 1976, 1977, and 1978 playoffs. I honestly did not know if life would go on after that. Of course, it eventually did. The Royals finally beat those darn Yankees in 1980 when George Brett hit his memorable home-run blastoff of Goose Gossage in game three of the American League Playoffs. Another disappointing loss soon came right after that in the 1980 World Series against the Philadelphia Phillies. My dad and I got to go to game three of that series, but Pete Rose and the Phillies beat our Kansas City Royals in six games.

In 1985, the Kansas City Royals pulled off two of the greatest comebacks in baseball history and rewarded Kansas City baseball fans with a world championship. Any frustrations from years past were quickly forgotten. Our beloved Royals were on top of the baseball world. The manner in which the Royals won it all that year was nothing short of amazing and inspiring. It seemed like all the unfortunate bad breaks and mishaps that had kept the Royals from winning a championship in the late '70s and early '80s reversed themselves in 1985. At the All-Star break, the Royals found themselves seven games out of first place and had to fight into the last week of the season to win the American League Western Division with a record of 91-71. Royals pitcher Bret Saberhagen won the Cy Young Award at the young age of just 21. In both the American League Championship Series and the World Series, the Royals had to battle back from a three-games-to-one deficit to win.

Having won 99 games during the regular season, the Toronto Blue Jays were heavy favorites to win the American League Championship Series against the Royals. After winning the first two games in Toronto, the favored Blue Jays certainly looked as if they would advance to the World Series. Game three would be played at Royals Stadium in Kansas City, Missouri. My dad and I had tickets to the game and were hoping we could turn the Royals' bad luck around. It had been five years since the last time Dad and I had gone to a playoff game together. I always loved going to sporting events with my dad. We always tried to manage the game together from the cheap seats. We discussed things like whether or not the Royals should bunt, play hit and run, or what guy out of the bullpen should be brought in to pitch. Early on, it looked as if we were good luck, as the Royals took a

2-0 lead going into the fifth inning. Disappointingly, Toronto then scored five runs in the top of the fifth to take a 5-2 lead. Then one of my all-time favorite Royals, George Brett, hit two home runs and turned the whole series and season around. The Royals came back to win game three 6-5, preventing a three-games-to-none deficit and keeping their slim World Series hopes alive.

The Blue Jays won game four in Kansas City by scoring three runs in the top of the ninth to win 3-1. That win gave them a commanding three-games-to-one advantage in the best-of-seven series. The Royals then proceeded to shock the baseball world by winning the last three games of the series. It was one of the greatest comebacks in American League Championship Series history. After winning game five at home, the Royals then traveled to Toronto and won game six 5-3 and game seven 6-2. The Royals won the series four games to three and were headed back to the World Series.

It was now off to the Show-Me-State Series where the Royals were once again   sizeable under-dogs. The St. Louis Cardinals had won 101 games during the regular season and were playing some of their best baseball. My dad and I were just hoping the series would go seven games because we had tickets to the seventh game. It did not look too promising after the first home games in Kansas City, however. St. Louis won game one 3-1, and game two 4-2.

Next, the Royals took their baseball show down I-70 east to St. Louis, Missouri. There, they won two out of the next three games, narrowing the Cardinals' lead to just three games to two. The Royals then returned home to Kansas City, needing just two wins for their first-ever World Championship.

Game six of the 1985 World Series is the game that will live in the hearts of Royals and Cardinals fans forever. The Cardinals were leading 1-0 going into the bottom of the ninth inning and were just three outs away from celebrating. Then Jorge Orta of the Royals hit a ball to the right side of the infield, where pitcher Todd Worrell was forced to cover first base. The television replay showed the ball clearly in Worrell's glove and his foot on the bag while Orta was still three feet short of reaching first base. The umpire called Orta safe, setting the stage for an improbable Royals victory. The Royals eventually scored two runs in the ninth, winning game six 2-1 and forcing a decisive seventh game.

Dad and I were headed off to game seven of the World Series together. We actually got to watch two sporting events that day because we had tickets to the Kansas City Chiefs game against the Denver Broncos earlier that Sunday. We went to the Chiefs game at noon and then walked across the parking lot for game seven of the World Series that night. I was practically in sports-fan heaven. We also cooked out and had a tailgate party between games, of course.

Game seven would be completely dominated by the Royals. Royals Cy Young winner Bret Saberhagen pitched a complete-game shutout as the Royals won 11-0, clinching Kansas City's first World Series championship. The St. Louis Cardinals weren't able to recover from the heartbreaking loss they had suffered in game six the night before. Years of frustrating losses erased, Kansas City finally sat on top of the baseball world. The Royals' victory set off a celebration in Kansas City that had not been seen since the Chiefs won Superbowl IV in 1969. My friends and I attended the Royals championship parade in downtown Kansas City later that week. This was one Royals victory I would celebrate in my heart for years.

The manager of the Royals in 1985 was Dick Howser. He managed the Kansas City Royals from 1981 to 1986. Dick Howser inspired me like no other Royal ever has by the courageous manner in which he battled brain cancer. Some people noticed that while managing the 1986 All-Star game, Howser began messing up signals when he changed pitchers. Howser later admitted that he had felt sick before the game. The All-Star game was the last game he would ever manage after being diagnosed with a brain tumor and immediately undergoing surgery. Howser fought cancer like a champion, even attempting a comeback with the Royals during spring training of 1987. He was too weak, however, and three months later, he died in St. Luke's Hospital in Kansas City. He was just 51 years of age.

It was hard for me to believe that one of my sports heroes could develop cancer and die so quickly. That was one of those moments in my life when I remember breaking down and crying. The courage and faith that Dick Howser and his wife showed in the face of death really had an impact on my life. I will never forget it. Dick Howser's death reminds me of the brevity and uncertainty of life. It reminded me that God has promised tomorrow to no man and that one's mountaintop moment can sometimes be followed by one's deepest valley. It also taught me that the manner in which we die can have a lasting impact on other people. I pray to God that when my turn to die comes, I will face death like a champion.

My senior year in high school, I made the decision that I would try out for the Truman High School wrestling team. I had worked out hard with weights for three years and had finally built up the confidence I needed to go out for the team. I weighed around 105 pounds my senior year. That was with my prosthetic legs off, of course. My upper body was really strong for someone who weighed only 105 pounds though. I could bench-press 110 pounds with just my left arm. Strength alone does not make a great wrestler, but dominating strength is a big help.

The coach of the Truman High School wrestling team was Ed Gensler. He had become the Truman coach in 1982. Coach Gensler had been quite a wrestler back in high school and college. He had placed second in the state of Missouri his senior year at North Kansas City High School in 1965. He had then gone on to wrestle at Graceland College in Lamoni, Iowa, where he won the conference tournament all four years. He was a tough guy whom I knew I would never want to mess with in a serious way, but Coach Gensler had a softer, friendlier side to him as well. He had a great sense of humor, and his knowledge of the sport of wrestling was impressive too. After college, he had refereed high school and college matches for ten years. I had a great deal of respect for Coach Gensler from the very beginning.

The first day of wrestling practice was memorable. Around 35 kids showed up for the first practice. By the time the real season started the final roster would have around half that number. There's probably no easier way to draw attention to yourself than to walk into a wrestling room and take your legs off in front of everyone. I can't think of a better way to kick off the wrestling season than that. I recall some of the questions of disbelief from the crowd of kids: "You're going to wrestle?" and "You're not here to try out for the team, are you?" I wanted to respond, "No, I'm just here to look pretty." To be honest, I had my share of doubts too. I knew I was a good athlete, though, and I knew God had given me quickness and a desire to compete. I was just hoping and praying it would be enough.

One of the first things you learn as a new wrestler is that strength and natural athletic ability are not as important as hard work, knowledge, and experience. The two areas I lacked the most were knowledge and experience. As a first-year wrestler, I was going to have to learn the sport very quickly. The more experienced wrestlers did not show mercy on us simply because we couldn't figure out which move to use. Wrestling is a lot about moves and proper technique. It is a lot like the game of chess: if you make one wrong move, it can be checkmate. I have watched in amazement as skinny guys with great technique destroy much stronger opponents with inferior wrestling skills. I have seen guys who could bench-press four hundred pounds who could not stay off their backs to save their lives.

In the 98-pound weight class, Truman returned one of its best young wrestling stars to come along in years, Jim Brewer. Jim would later go onto become a four- time state qualifier and to win the Missouri State Championship his senior year. His junior year, he would lose in the state final by only one point, narrowly missing being a two-time state champion.

The 105-pound weight class was a wide-open horse race. There were three of us trying out for the 105-pound varsity spot. Fortunately, neither of the guys I was competing against had a lot of experience either. I knew I had to make the varsity team if I was going to get an opportunity to wrestle, however. They had a rule in high school wrestling that a senior could not wrestle junior varsity, so the pressure was on me to beat both guys in my weight class. I was just glad I wasn't seven pounds lighter and having to knock the state qualifier, Jim Brewer, out of his spot to make the varsity team. I had heard all the scary rumors about Jim Brewer and how good he was. I was relieved that we weren't in the same weight class.

Coach Gensler's practices were tough. They were designed to either get you into shape or kill you, whichever came first. Six minutes on a wrestling mat can easily feel like six months when you are up against someone quicker, stronger, and more talented than you are. Coach Gensler understood that reality. There were times when many of us probably hated Coach Gensler for pushing us so hard, but obviously, he knew what he was doing. Once the season started, we would all be happy that Gensler's practices were so demanding. Wrestling is not an easy sport. Just ask the football players who would stop by the wrestling room after football practice. I recall several guys with overblown egos coming in and challenging some of our top wrestlers to a match. After being thrown on their backs in a matter of seconds, the football players were usually more than ready to go back to their much more familiar game of blocking and tackling.

We started each practice with a lot of stretching. It's important to stretch properly to prevent injuries in wrestling. Then we did a lot of running. Most of the guys went out into the hallways in the school to run laps. I just stayed in the wrestling room and ran on my knees on the two large wrestling mats that we had rolled out. Running serves as great cross-training for wrestling. You have to be in excellent cardiovascular shape to win a wrestling match.

Coach Gensler would have us break up into groups of four and work on different wrestling moves. Having only one out of four limbs, I was not able to do many of the moves that we worked on in practice. I didn't let that bother me, though. I just focused on the moves that I could execute and tried to at least understand the ones that I could not execute. Coach Gensler told me that if I could just master three or four key moves, I would do just fine.

My favorite and most effective move was the single-leg takedown. My left arm was strong and extremely quick. Many times, my opponents were off balance while trying to get at me and would leave their legs open for the taking. I usually tried to take my opponents down to the mat using the single-leg takedown and then tried to catch them on their backs.

If I could catch them on their backs, many times, I would be able to use my dominating strength and pin them. I went on to win quite a few matches that way.

The weakest part of my wrestling game was when I was in the bottom position. I had a difficult time escaping from the bottom because I didn't have legs to stand up and hadn't developed enough high-quality moves to allow me to escape. It was critical for me to be able to take my opponents down. More often than not, if I could not take my opponent down, I would not win the match. My best move from the bottom position was to kick my hips out and do what is called a sit-out. This would allow me to face my opponent and earn one point for an escape. My bottom game certainly needed a lot of work, however. My strategy was normally to try to stay out of the bottom position to begin with. When I did find myself in the bottom position, it usually took every ounce of my energy to get out.

After our practice in groups of four, Coach Gensler would have us do takedown drills. Everyone would take turns in the center of the wrestling mat as other wrestlers were sent out to try and take them down. Coach would blow the whistle, and we would have one minute to try to find any legal way possible to score a two-point takedown against our opponent. When it was my turn to be in the center, the first opponent I usually faced was 98-pound state qualifier Jim Brewer. To my surprise, I generally held my own against Jim in takedown drills. I believe the reason for that was the short duration of the drills. My problems against Jim Brewer normally came the longer I was on the mat with him. I could hold him off for only so long. He was eventually going to get me. The second guy sent out against me was normally our returning 112-pound varsity letterman, Glenn Gross. He was tough, too. There were no easy roads in high school wrestling. (Trust me: there were days I looked for one.) After facing Glenn Gross, I would face our 119-pound varsity wrestler, Danny Hughes. I don't think I was ever able to take Danny down. I came close a few times with single-leg takedown shots, but Danny had great balance and would hop on one leg to escape trouble or get out of bounds. Danny Hughes ended up a four-year varsity letterman and would later defeat a guy who placed fifth in the state of Missouri. Going up against talented guys like Danny quickly helped raise my wrestling skills to another level.

The time for team tryouts arrived. I was hoping that I had done enough to be prepared to beat both guys in my weight class and represent my school in the 105-pound varsity spot. I had put in all the hard work and had trusted the instruction of my coaches. Now it was just a matter of executing and making it happen. It was show time. The first guy I went up against was a first-year high school wrestler like me. He had wrestled a couple of years in junior high but not at the high school level. My thinking going into the match was that I wanted to end it as quickly as possible. I figured the longer the match went on, the greater chance I had of making a mistake and getting beat. Coach Gensler blew the whistle, and I immediately shot in for a single-leg takedown. My high school wrestling career had officially begun. My first shot proved to be right on target, and I was able to take my opponent down to the mat. Without hesitation, I pounced right on him and was able to catch him on his back. I then quickly went after a first-period pin. Seconds later, Coach Gensler pounded the mat, signaling that I was victorious! I had won my first high school wrestling match by pin in less than one minute! It was clearly a great start, but I couldn't get too excited: I had one big match down but still had one bigger match to go.

I went into my second match with the same mentality as I had in the first: I did not want the match to get out of the first period if I could help it. The second wrestler I faced was a little stronger than the first guy. He had clearly spent some time in the weight room pumping iron. He had limited wrestling experience, however, and that made him another good match for me. Once again, Gensler blew the whistle to begin the match. To my surprise, my opponent shot in on me, but luckily, I was able to catch him in a front headlock. The front headlock was a move that worked a lot for me against inexperienced wrestlers. From that position, I would do a front headlock roll and try to catch my opponent's arm to put him on his back. Then all I would do was squeeze as hard as I could around his neck and look up. Looking up is critical for a successful pin. Many beginning wrestlers make the mistake of looking down at the mat to see if the other guy's shoulder blades are pinned. That mistake can cost you a match if you're not careful. I had learned that lesson early on, so in this match, I looked straight up in the air, hoping to finish it. Coach Gensler circled the mat on his hands and knees, trying to get a good look. Then he pounded the mat, indicating that I had pinned my second straight opponent, kicking off my first wrestling career celebration. I had won my first two high school wrestling matches by pinning both of my opponents in less than a minute! I had made the varsity wrestling team as a first-year wrestler and would represent Truman High School as their 105-pound varsity wrestler!

Jim Brewer and I became pretty good friends over the course of the wrestling season. I think early on, we had a mutual respect for each other's athletic ability. Some might find it hard to believe that you could be friends with a guy who tried to take your head off at practice each day, but Jim and I both understood the nature of the sport we were engaged in. Wrestling against one of the best wrestlers in the state every day allowed me to improve in a hurry. Jim Brewer was only a sophomore in high school but was in his eighth year of wrestling. He taught me a lot of moves and techniques that I could have never learned on my own. He was extremely strong, too: he competed in the 98-pound weight class but could bench-press 180 pounds!

Jim and I had several things in common, including our love for food. That love for food would put us into a little dilemma going into our first wrestling tournament. Jim was having trouble getting down to his 98-pound weight class, so Coach Gensler had Jim and me wrestle for the 105-pound spot. Coach Gensler's team coaching philosophy was that all varsity wrestling spots were always up for grabs. Each week, anyone could challenge anyone else for their spot, and if they won, they would take that place in the lineup. No one was ever safe. It was good, though, because it made us always want to get better to protect our places on the team. Wrestling Jim Brewer would allow me to find out where I was on my wrestling journey. I was just a first-year wrestler going up against a future state champion with eight years of wrestling experience. I probably should have been scared, but for some reason, I wasn't. I knew it was going to be tough, but I went into my match with Jim hoping to win. I always hoped to win. That is the only way to compete in sports: You have to believe!

Everyone on the wrestling team gathered around to watch Jim and me wrestle off for the 105-pound varsity spot. Wrestling matches in high school were six minutes long; three two-minute periods. I couldn't take the same philosophy into the match against Jim that I had taken into my two prior 105-pound matches. In both of those matches, I was able to physically overpower my opponents and pin them early in the match. In a match against Jim, I had to figure out how to score more points than he did. My mindset was to take the match one period at a time. I tried to divide the match into three separate two-minute matches. If I could find a way to win two out of the three periods, then I might be able to pull off the upset.

Coach Gensler blew the whistle, and the match began. Jim and I came out extremely aggressive. We were both in the stand-up position, and I kept trying to pull his head down and knock him off balance. I put my left hand behind his head and pulled down as hard as I could. To my surprise, Jim lost his balance for a split second, allowing me to shoot in on a single-leg takedown. My shot was successful, and I took an early 2-0 lead in the match. Moments later, though, Jim did a quick reversal and tied the score at 2-2. I was now in the bottom position, which was rarely a good place for me. Jim did his best to ride out the rest of the first period on top, but with only a few seconds left I was able to score a one-point escape. The score at the end the first period was 3-2. The good news was that I had just won the first period against one of the best wrestlers in the state. The bad news was that I still had two long two-minute periods to go. That was an eternity against a guy like Jim Brewer.

I had my choice of starting position to begin the second period and chose to start in the down position. My thinking was that if I could keep Jim from turning me over onto my back, I could go into the final period with a 3-2 lead. Turning me over on my back was difficult because of my upper-body strength. Jim understood that and immediately let me escape early in the second period. My lead in the match was now 4-2.

One of Jim's best moves was the Olympic head-lock. I would watch him win many of his matches with the Olympic headlock. The problem for Jim's opponents was in preventing him from executing the move and effectively countering it. I always knew to look for the Olympic headlock, but stopping it proved to be easier said than done. With around a minute left in the second period, Jim threw me onto my back using his favorite Olympic headlock move. Jim liked that move for several reasons, but one of the biggest was that it was a five-point move. He got not only two points for a takedown but three points for putting his opponent on his back. I had to fight for my life the last minute of the second period just to keep from being pinned. I went from being ahead 4-2 to being behind 7-4. The match had changed dramatically on just one big move.

In the third period, Jim chose the neutral stand-up position. I had to try to get my head back into the match in a hurry after giving up a five-point move. I still had a chance to win, but I needed to take Jim down and put him on his back; a position that Jim Brewer rarely ever found himself in. Coach Gensler blew the whistle, and I went right after Jim. Getting thrown on my back had not made me a happy wrestler. One quick lesson you learn in wrestling, as well as all sports, is that you have to control your emotions. Keeping your cool when things go against you is critical. I was probably too aggressive going after Jim, and I quickly found myself on my back again. I spent the last minute and a half of the match trying not to get pinned. I ended up losing my match against my friend, 12-4. I was disappointed, but I was able to take a lot of positives from the loss. I now knew that I could compete with some of the best wrestlers in the state. I also knew that I had a lot to learn but that I would enter the wrestling season with much to be optimistic about.

We opened the new wrestling season with a tournament at Ruskin High School. Jim was still cutting weight and was down to 101 pounds. He would be our 105-pound varsity wrestler for the opening tournament. Jim would be down to his 98-pound weight class by the following weekend, allowing me to wrestle varsity at 105 pounds. In the meantime, Coach Gensler decided to set up an exhibition match for me against a guy from Hickman Mills High School. Coach thought that an exhibition match would help give me some good experience and help me get over some of my early-season anxieties.

I have to admit, I was very nervous going into my first wrestling match, even if it was just an exhibition. Looking at the guy I was going to wrestle, though, I believe he was just as nervous as I was. I believe that, to some extent, my disability may have given me a psychological advantage over some of my opponents too. I honestly don't know how I might handle wrestling someone missing three limbs. It definitely could mess with someone's head a little.

The referee blew the whistle, and my first real high school wrestling match began. The first thirty seconds of the match were intense. We both took turns trying single- and double-leg takedown shots on each other. My opponent was almost able to get the first takedown, but fortunately, we were on the edge of the mat and I was able to get out of bounds. When we came back to the center of the mat for the restart, I faked another single-leg takedown move. When the Hickman Mills wrestler came down to block my shot, I was able to catch him in a front headlock and take him to his back. After that, all I can remember is hearing my teammates shouting with excitement and, moments later, the referee pounding the mat. I had won my first high school wrestling match by way of pin!

The following weekend, Truman High School would host a wrestling tournament of its own. I would get to kick off my varsity-wrestling career in my home school and in front of my fellow students. To say that I was excited would be an understatement. Seven other schools would come to Truman with their best wrestlers to battle it out for first place. The tournament would be spread out over two days: Friday night and Saturday afternoon. Friday night, I was scheduled to wrestle the 105-pound varsity guy from Ruskin High School. Jim Brewer gave a full scouting report on the guy that had me concerned even before the match began. Jim had had an extremely difficult time beating this Ruskin kid the year before in a match. I knew going in I was going to have to perform well if I hoped to win.

The referee signaled for us to come to the center of the mat, had us shake hands, and then blew the whistle to get the match started. I could tell from the beginning that it was going to be a tough match. The guy I was up against was strong and very intense. I figured early on that I would probably need to go six minutes if I was going to win. About a minute into the match, my opponent scored the first takedown by knocking me off balance. I had to decide quickly to give up the two-point takedown and go to my stomach to prevent him from putting me on my back for additional points. I spent the last minute trying everything I could imagine trying to get out from the bottom position. The first period came to an end with me stuck on bottom and trailing 2-0.

I looked over to Coach to see where he wanted me to start the second period. He pointed down, so I started the second period right where I ended the first, on bottom. It turned out to be the right call, as thirty seconds into the second period, I scored a one-point escape and narrowed my deficit to just 2-1. It didn't take my opponent long, though, before he shot in on me again and scored another two-point take-down, giving him a 4-1 lead. He then rode me for the rest of the second period, taking his 4-1 lead into the third period.

My opponent chose to start the third period in the down position. Coach then signaled me to let him up and to go for a takedown and back points. The score was 5-1, and I had only two minutes to prevent myself from losing my opening varsity wrestling match. My opponent quickly shot in on me again, and I caught him in a front headlock. I tried to roll him onto his back, but this guy was too experienced. He just rolled right through it and came right back to his stomach again. I eventually had to push him away and go back to a neutral position with him. He then did a duck-under move against me and was able to score a two-point takedown, giving him a commanding 7-1 lead. I was able to score one more escape before the match ended but still lost my first varsity match by the score of 7-2. I was a little discouraged. Coach Gensler seemed to be pretty satisfied by my opening performance. Coach knew the Ruskin guy was a tough varsity wrestler because he had seen him against Jim the year before, so he told me to keep my head up because good things were going to happen to me. That particular Ruskin wrestler would end up qualifying for the state tournament later that same year.

I went home that Friday evening and tried to heal physically and emotionally before coming back on Saturday to wrestle three more matches. I was pretty beat-up after my match with the guy from Ruskin Friday night. He had dragged me all over the mat, trying to turn me over for back points. I had a big piece of skin missing on my right elbow that hurt like nothing I had ever felt before. Turning around and coming right back to wrestle the next day around noon was a challenge.

My first match on Saturday was against a kid from St. Joe Lafayette. I kind of felt like I had let my team down the night before, so I came out wanting to show everyone that I was there to win. When the match began, I didn't waste any time before taking my first shot. I picked up one of my opponent's legs and threw him down onto the mat. He fell onto his back, and I was able to catch him there. He fought hard off his back, however, and was able to keep from getting pinned. The referee awarded me two points for a takedown and three back points, giving me a 5-0 early lead. My opponent then made a critical mistake when he tried a sit-out move without first clearing his arm. He basically put himself on his back again for me, and that time, I was able to pin him. I had won my first varsity match with a first-period pin! The victory allowed me to score the maximum number of points for my team and made me feel a whole lot better than I had after losing the night before. Coach Gensler and my teammates seemed happier for me than I was. It was great to feel like an important member of the team.

My second match on Saturday was against one of the toughest wrestlers in the state at 105 pounds. Jim told me a lot about this tough kid from William Chrisman High School that I would have to face. He kind of looked to me like Sylvester Stallone in the movie *Rocky III.* I had never known you could pack so much muscle on a 105- pound frame. I was a little bit intimidated going into this match. Coach Gensler told me that I was just as big and strong as he was and to just wrestle my own game, so to speak. This was one time I didn't believe Coach.

The referee blew the whistle, and I immediately tried to grab one of my opponent's ankles to pick it up. I missed, and he spun around behind me for a two-point takedown. We were just seconds into the match, and I was already behind, 2-0. I remember going much of the rest of the first period just trying to move. When I finally was able to get some room to move around a little, I walked into a move that I did not even know could be used against me. My opponent put me into a cradle even though I barely had any legs below my knees. In practice, the coaches and I had gone over this move and had determined that I could not fall victim to it because I didn't have enough legs below my knees to make it work. We had been wrong. My opponent not only got me into a cradle but he ended up pinning me with it late in the first period. I couldn't believe it. I had just enough leg below my left knee for my opponent to sink in a cradle and hook my left leg, giving me no way to escape. The match was quickly over and was certainly not a fun way to learn a valuable lesson. The only consolation for me was that that particular Chrisman wrestler would also qualify for the state tournament later in the year.

My final match of the tournament on Saturday was against a guy from Rockhurst High School. Rockhurst was known around Kansas City for being a powerhouse football school, but it also had a pretty good wrestling team. I wanted badly to finish the tournament on a winning note and earn my team some valuable points and help us move up in the overall tournament standings.

The referee started us off, and my opponent faked a shot at me. When I went down to block him, he caught me in a front headlock. I had used that move so often myself that I knew how to counter it. My opponent tried to roll me over to my back, but I didn't allow him to catch my arm, and I just rolled right on through it. I then pulled out of the headlock and used my own version of a move called a duck-under that allowed me to spin behind for the first takedown of the match. From the top position, I was able to turn my opponent over to his back and earn an additional three back points. At the end of the first period I was ahead 5-0.

The kid from Rockhurst chose the down position to begin the second period. Coach Gensler felt confident in my ability to take my opponent down, so he signaled for me to let him up and give him one point for an escape. Coach was right, and moments later, I shot in on a single-leg takedown and was able to put my opponent on his back again. I was able to hold him on his back until the end of the second period and enter the third period with a 10-1 lead.

Coach had me start the third period in the down position. My opponent from Rockhurst needed a lot of points or a pin to win so he decided to let me up and give me a one-point escape. That extended my lead to 11-1. There was a rule in high school wrestling that if you got ahead by 15 points or more, the match would be over so at that point, all I needed was one more five-point move to finish the match. I shot in on another single-leg takedown move and was able to take my opponent down once again. I wasn't able to keep him on his back to get back points, however. The score was now 13-1, and I still needed three more points to win. I then put in what is known as a chicken-wing move and was able to get my opponent onto his back for three additional points. The final score of the match was 16-1. I had finished my first varsity-wrestling tournament with a record of 2-2 and had finished in fifth place.

After the Truman tournament, the *Kansas City Star* came out to our high school to do a story on me. They interviewed Coach Gensler, Jim Brewer, and myself for the article. I was honestly amazed that anyone thought that what I was doing was newsworthy. I was just doing what came naturally and what I loved to do. I loved to compete, and I loved to win. God had blessed me with some athletic talent and a passion for sports, and wrestling provided an arena for me to display those gifts.

Unfortunately, a little later in the season an injury to my right knee brought a close to my high school wrestling career. It was very disappointing, because my high school wrestling story was sort of left unfinished. I had felt like I was just beginning to understand the sport of wrestling and it would have been nice to see how far I could have gone in the tournament at the end of the year. Some people believed that I had the potential to be a state qualifier in my very first year if I had kept improving. I honestly don't know. All of that is speculation, of course.

Despite my shortened season, I was still able to earn a varsity letter as a first-year wrestler and have a .500 record. Wrestling taught me many lessons that I've carried with me throughout my life such as discipline and a strong work ethic. I really enjoyed being a part of a team as well. I liked all of my teammates and everyone cheered for and respected each other. Everyone wanted to see everyone else succeed. There was a sort of fraternity or brotherhood that you joined when you became a wrestler. We knew what the others were going through out there on the mat, and we became fellow warriors. When I went to a wrestling meet, I got the sense that we were going into battle together. Wrestling also provided me with a foundation for an exciting athletic career. High school wrestling was only the beginning.

CHAPTER 3

When Life Hands You a Lemon, Trust God

Going through life missing three limbs has had its share of challenges, but it didn't take me long when I look around the world to see that plenty of people have been dealt tougher cards than I have been. Life is not fair. I learned that lesson early in life. God doesn't buy into the fairness doctrine. God gives one man a body like Michael Jordan and then gives another man one arm and no legs. What's up with that? What are you supposed to do with that? Let me tell you what you don't do with that; throw a pity party. Trust me, I have thrown more than my fair share of pity parties over the years, and they're never much fun. God never seems to show up for my pity parties, either, no matter how hard I cry.

It took me a while, but I finally figured out why God never showed up. My pity parties didn't have any faith. Hebrews 11:6 says, "And without faith it is impossible to please God, because anyone who comes to him must believe that he exists and that he rewards those who earnestly seek Him." The Bible says that the

God who created this universe is a God of faith. A pity party says to God, "My problems are too big for you," but faith says, "With God, all things are possible!" God is moved by faith.

Faith is many times a misunderstood word. Hebrews 11:1 defines faith: "Now faith is being sure of what we hope for and certain of what we do not see." Notice it says that faith is being certain of what we do not see. The scary part about faith is that it requires us to believe without first seeing. If you could see it, it wouldn't be faith. I heard a great explanation of faith told in a story about a famous tightrope walker who strung a wire across Niagara Falls. A great crowd began to gather as he started to walk across the wire. When he made it to the other side he turned to the crowd and asked them, "How many of you believe that I can put a man on my back and walk across this wire across Niagara Falls?" Most of the crowd nodded, saying they indeed believed that he could carry a man across on his back. So he then turned to the crowd while pointing to one man and said, "You, get on my back." Real faith takes action and is not just a mental affirmation. The kind of faith that pleases God is the kind that climbs onto the man's back believing to be carried across. Is it scary? Yes! Faith takes courage and that is why the Bible recognizes heroes of the faith. They jumped knowing that God would catch them. Romans 1:17 says, "The righteous will live by faith."

Sometimes in life it's easy to get overwhelmed by our problems and think that there is no hope. One thing I have had to admit through my many mistakes in life is that God is a just a tad bit smarter than I am and His solutions to my problems are far superior to anything I can come up with on my own. I think sometimes we tend to forget that it was God who created our brains, and not the other way around. God is far wiser and smarter than many people realize. I believe God can take the absolute worst of circumstances and turn them completely around for our good and His glory. Perhaps the greatest example in history of this is the cross of Christ. God took the cross, an instrument of death used by the Romans to execute thousands of people in the cruelest fashion, and turned it into an instrument of love to save the world. If God is capable of that, surely He can take my seemingly insurmountable problems and turn them around for good. Proverbs 3:5-6 says, "Trust in the Lord with all your heart and lean not on your own understanding; in all your ways acknowledge Him, and He will make your paths straight." When life hands you a lemon, trust God.

A lady whose life has inspired me for years is Joni Eareckson Tada. Her example of trusting God in the face of some of the most difficult circumstances imaginable has been an inspiration to millions all over the world. Joni was born October 15, 1949, in Baltimore, Maryland. She was the youngest of four sisters and grew up very happy and active. She liked riding horses and loved to swim. At the age of 17, she went to the beach on Chesapeake Bay to swim with her sister and some friends. In a split second, her life changed forever. She dove head first into the shallow water and broke her neck between the fourth and fifth cervical vertebrae. Her sister Kathy rescued her and had her taken by ambulance to the hospital. The devastating news to follow changed the course of Joni's life forever. She was paralyzed from the shoulders down, a quadriplegic. She spent the next several months in the hospital, fighting for her life and trying to come to grips with the fact that she would have to spend the rest of her life in a wheelchair.

Joni struggled to understand why God had let something so horrible happen to her and what she could have done to deserve her new reality. She spent months fighting depression and the desire to end her life after the tragic accident. Or was it really an accident? Could it be possible that it had been no accident at all? Prior to the accident, Joni had asked God to change her life because she felt like she wasn't living the type of life she thought she should be living. Over time, Joni began to wonder if somehow this could have been God's answer to her prayer. Could God allow something so horrible to come into one of His children's lives in order to bring about something glorious with eternal significance? Could God possibly be that intelligent and that awesome? Could God be that cruel, one might ask. Joni Eareckson Tada has said many great things over the years, but one of my favorites is "Sometimes God allows what he hates to accomplish what he loves." As time went by, Joni began to see her new set of circumstances in a completely different light than she had immediately after her paralysis. She would later say, "We will stand amazed to see the topside of the tapestry and how God beautifully embroidered each circumstance into a pattern for our good and His glory."

After her two years of rehabilitation, Joni became a public speaker and began working to help other people with disabilities. Today, Joni is a Christian author, a radio host, and the founder of Joni and Friends. Joni and Friends is a Christian organization that ministers to the disabled throughout the world. Joni is also an artist: she learned how to paint with a brush between her teeth.

Though Joni has indicated that she believes there is no inherent goodness in disability or disease, she does believe that God can turn any difficulty or tragedy into something good for us and into glory for Himself. She has come to believe that God clearly had a motive and a purpose for her disability. She said that prior to her accident, her values had been upside down. She had thought like many people that life was all about looking good, having plenty of creature comforts like a beautiful house and a nice car, and getting married and having 2.5 kids. After her accident, the things that really mattered to her were friendships and love: love between a husband and a wife or with a sister, brother, niece, or neighbor. She began to realize that people counted the most. She began to cherish the smiles, tears, and embraces she shared with loved ones.

Joni has written more than forty books on the topics of Christianity and disability. She has been inducted into the Christian Booksellers Association's Hall of Honor. Over the years, Tada has won the Victory Award from the National Rehabilitation

Hospital, the Award of Excellence from the Patricia Neal Rehabilitation Center, the Courage Award from the Courage Rehabilitation Center, the Golden Word Award from the International Bible Society, and the Golden Plate Award from the American Academy of Achievement. Tada received the William Ward Ayer Award for excellence from the National Religious Broadcasters Association in 2002. She was awarded the Gold Medallion Award for the book *When God Weeps* in 2003. She won the Gold Medallion Award for coauthoring *Hymns for a Kid's Heart*, Volume 1 in 2004. In 2005, Joni was appointed to the Disability Advisory Committee of the U.S. State Department. Tada was also inducted into Indiana Wesleyan University's Society of World Changers in 2009. Today, she serves on a number of advisory boards and has received honorary graduate degrees from colleges, universities, and seminaries.

I could not begin to imagine the challenges and suffering that Joni Eareckson Tada has had to endure since becoming paralyzed. My disability pales in comparison to being a quadriplegic. Though I may be missing three limbs, all of my body parts move and function normally. I thank God for Joni's example and ministry. She has been a shining light to countless people in the world who had given up on life, believing there was no hope. Despite her many sufferings, Joni's life has impacted millions of lives and has had eternal significance.

The most famous example of a person trusting God when life handed him a lemon was demonstrated in the life of Job in the Old Testament. Job was a God-fearing man who lived in the land of Uz. He had seven sons and three daughters. He was a very righteous and blessed man. He owned several thousand sheep and camels and was the greatest man in the East.

The story of Job is helpful to look at because it can give us insight into the age-old question "Why do bad things happen to good people?" Science and modern technology many times can tell us what happens, but to get to the issue of why things happen, we have to dig a whole lot deeper. Sometimes circumstances that seem simple on the surface can be much more complicated than they appear. Isaiah 55:8-9 says, "For my thoughts are not your thoughts, neither are your ways my ways, declares the Lord. As the heavens are higher than the earth, so are my ways higher than your ways, and my thoughts than your thoughts." One of the major themes of the Book of Job is that tragedy and suffering are not merely punishment for wrongdoing but can be used by God as trials or as discipline to result in spiritual growth.

The Book of Job starts out with an interesting little challenge from God to Satan. (Notice that God initiated the confrontation.) Job 1:8-12 says, "Then the Lord said to Satan, 'Have you considered my servant Job? There is no one on earth like him; he is blameless and upright, a man who fears God and shuns evil.' 'Does Job fear God for nothing?' Satan replied. 'Have you not put a hedge around him and his household and everything he has? You have blessed the work of his hands, so that his flocks and herds are spread throughout the land. But stretch out your hand and strike everything he has, and he will surely curse you to your face.' The Lord said to Satan, 'Very well, then, everything he has is in your hands, but on the man himself do not lay a finger.'" Notice that Satan is on a leash; he can do only what God allows him to do.

Job loses all of his livestock to thieves, and all of his children are killed when a house collapses on them in a windstorm. After going through all of that, Job does not curse God or accuse Him of any wrongdoing. God's not finished yet, however. God soon comes back and initiates round two with Satan.

In Job 2:3-6, the confrontation continues. "Then the Lord said to Satan, 'Have you considered my servant Job? There is no one on earth like him; he is blameless and upright, a man who fears God and shuns evil. And he still maintains his integrity, though you incited me against him to ruin him without any reason.' 'Skin for skin!' Satan replied. 'A man will give all he has for his own life. But strike out your hand and strike his flesh and bones, and he will surely curse you to your face.' The Lord said to Satan, 'Very well, then, he is in your hands; but you must spare his life.'"

So then Satan afflicts Job with painful sores all over his body. Still, Job does not curse God or accuse him of any wrongdoing. Job's three friends have heard about all of his sufferings and come from far away to comfort him. Job finally starts to show signs of cracking when he begins to curse the day of his birth, but he still never curses God.

We can learn many lessons from Job's incredible example of trusting God no matter what life brings. The first thing that we see Job do after he loses his children and all of his wealth is praise God. Job 1:21 says, "Naked I came from my mother's womb, and naked I will depart. The Lord gave and the Lord has taken away; may the name of the Lord be praised." Job was an extremely wise man who understood the game of life more than most people. I believe that is what made it possible for Job to stand under ridiculous pressure and not break. Job, for example, understood that everything he had was a gift from God. Job knew full well that what God gives, God can take away.

Job also knew that God was sovereign in his life and that nothing came into his life unless God allowed it. Over thirty times in the Book of Job, God is called "the Almighty." We are constantly reminded in the Book of Job that God is in control of everything. When you know that an all-powerful, all-knowing, all-loving God is in control of all of your life's circumstances, it makes it possible to trust Him even when it may appear to be hopeless. Job did not fully know God's hidden purpose for the things he was suffering, but he had faith to believe that God was working it all out for good.

Job's wisdom came from the fact that he feared God. Proverbs 9:10 says, "The fear of the Lord is the beginning of wisdom, and knowledge of the Holy One is understanding." Fearing the Lord means having a respect for who He is and what He says. Oswald Chambers once said, "The remarkable thing about fearing God is that when you fear God, you fear nothing else: whereas if you do not fear God, you fear everything else."

Job's wisdom caused him to ask questions like "What can I get out of this situation?" instead of what most of us tend to ask: "How can I get out of this situation?" Job knew that an all-loving God was behind the curtain, and knowing that allowed him to keep going when others would have quit.

Job's friends had their own ideas about why Job was suffering. They believed Job's suffering was due to his own sin in his life, which was completely contrary to what God had said about Job. God had said that Job was blameless and upright. Job's friends basically told Job that he was a sinner, that he was hiding his sins, and that if he wanted God to restore him, he needed to repent. Their entire theology was centered on the fact that God is just and if someone suffers, the person must have done something to deserve it. Job's friends were wrong, of course, but they were so set on their own preconceived ideas of how God works that they failed to recognize that God is far too big to fit into a simple little box. Job's friends brought their own experiences and presuppositions with them and could see things only from their own perspective.

The main reason for Job's suffering, as it turns out, was to prove the accusations of Satan false and to demonstrate that a man would indeed honor God even though he had lost his health, his wealth, and his children. At stake in Job's life was the answer to a very important universal question: "Is God worthy of man's worship even when life hands him a lemon?" Job answered that question with a resounding yes! God is worthy of our worship, no matter what life brings us. Satan's basic argument that God had to pay people to worship Him was refuted! Job's example of trusting God despite losing everything speaks through the centuries to all of us that we, too, can trust God amidst our darkest and loneliest moments in life. Even if we don't understand all that is going on around us, we can rest assured that an all-powerful, all-knowing, all-loving God is in control of all of life's circumstances and will work it all out for good. We can always trust God to do the right thing, no matter how difficult our situation might be.

In the end, God restored Job and gave him twice as much as he had before. God gave him seven sons and three daughters. God blessed the latter part of Job's life more than the beginning. Job would have 14,000 sheep, 6,000 camels, a 1,000 yoke of oxen, and 1,000 donkeys. He lived 140 years and then died old and full of days.

It was the fall of 1986 and I was entering my freshman year at the University of Kansas in Lawrence, Kansas. I started college thinking that I was going to study to be a mechanical engineer. I honestly had no idea what I wanted to do for a career, so mechanical engineering sounded like as good a major as any to start out in. At least engineers were usually in demand and made a pretty decent living. My parents wanted me to have an excellent place to live while going away to school, so they paid for me to stay at Naismith Hall, a dorm close to campus that provided everything I would need to succeed. When

I had come to visit the K.U. campus in Lawrence in the summer of 1986, I had immediately fallen in love with it. I couldn't believe how beautiful it was and how it just felt like its own city within a city. I was excited about the new college journey that I was about to begin.

Going away to college and being away from Mom and Dad for the first time was a new experience for me. It was my first taste of living on my own, and it brought with it many opportunities as well as distractions. Naismith Hall was a co-ed dorm, and there were lots of pretty girls to divert a young man's attention from what he should be doing, like studying. As I look back, I'm amazed that I made it through college with all the temptations that there were. I estimate that a quarter of my friends did not make it past the first semester because of failing grades. I chalk the key to my survival up to the grace of almighty God. I believe when I attended K.U., the graduation rate for freshmen was around 50%. There are a lot of casualties on the road to earning the much-coveted college degree.

I had four classes my first semester at K.U.: economics, calculus, English, and history. My classes were spread out all over the campus in different buildings and at different times. That would take some getting used to and create plenty of challenges. Obviously back in high school, all I had to do was make it into one building every day. In college, many times, I would need to go to five or six different buildings in a day. Getting around a university campus can be a challenge for people with all of their limbs, let alone for a triple amputee. I would ride the bus all over campus and would be dropped off somewhat close to the building where my class was. Then I would still need to walk a great distance for many of my classes. It was extremely challenging in the wintertime when the sidewalks were full of ice and snow. Walking on ice or snow with prosthetic legs can be downright scary sometimes because you don't know when the ground is going to be pulled out from underneath you. I cannot count the number of times I have unwillingly done the splits when my legs have just suddenly slid out from underneath me. It happens so quickly that I don't even know what has happened until I'm on the ground. Thank God I have yet to get injured in a fall.

After classes, I usually went back to the dorm and ate lunch in the cafeteria. The cafeteria at Naismith Hall had excellent food and a wide variety of meals to choose from. It's a good thing that I stayed physically active, or I would have put on at least twenty pounds living there. After lunch, I often went back to the recreation room in the dorm. The recreation room had about seven or eight video game machines we could put our quarters in and play. The dorm also had a pool table, a table tennis table, and a weight room. I was a pretty decent pool player because I had grown up with a pool table in our basement at home. I would normally play some pool and lift some weights after lunch.

It was at Naismith Hall that a friend by the name of Rich Maney who was living on my floor introduced me to the sport of table tennis. Rich was from New

Jersey and was an excellent tennis and table tennis player. Watching him play, I immediately wanted to emulate him. One evening after dinner, I went down and watched my friend beat five other guys in the dorm with very little effort. At that moment, I knew I had found my new sport for life. Table tennis would go onto become my favorite sport and a tremendous blessing. I knew from the beginning that I would be good at table tennis because I had good hand-eye coordination and I was quick. Table tennis doesn't force one to run to be successful like tennis does, either. Obviously, one has to be able to move enough to cover the table: with prosthetic legs, I was able to do so. It took me about two years of playing before I was able to win some matches from my friend from New Jersey. We went on to have some very hard-fought close matches with each other.

In the latter half of my freshman year at K.U., I also took up the sport of running. I had run around on my knees my whole life and had run short distances to get in shape for sports like wrestling. For the first time, I began running miles and timing myself. I simply turned a shoe around backward to cover my left knee and had a special pad to cover my right knee. It wasn't long before I set a goal to run a 10k on my knees in less than 1.5 hours. My training would lead to a 10k race that I would run in the spring of my sophomore year. The details of that race are described in Chapter 7, "Do You Believe in Miracles?"

My second year at K.U. forced me to get serious about deciding what I really wanted to do for a career.

I was starting to enter some of the real meat of the mechanical engineering curriculum and found out real quickly that I was in way over my head. I was really good at math so my calculus classes never gave me any trouble. My downfall was science and more specifically, physics. I had gotten a B in my chemistry class my freshman year, but physics was absolutely killing me. I remember being up late at night, working story problems that literally made me want to start crying. I kept looking in the back of the book for the answers, but they weren't there. It was ultimately one of my engineering classes that put me over the edge and forced me to make a career change.

One of my engineering classes was called Science of Materials. I remember walking into Strong Hall, the engineering building at K.U., and being completely intimidated by all the smart-looking people. I experienced a one-hour lecture in my Science of Materials class that made me decide to pursue a degree in business instead of engineering. The first thing I recall about the class was that I was surrounded by Asian-Americans, one on each side of me. Many Asian-Americans become wonderful engineers because they are brilliant. I discovered real quickly that I did not have the type of intellect to be an engineer. I have much more of a business mind than an engineering mind. That Science of Materials class was the only time in my academic life when I honestly can say, I sat through an entire lecture and did not understand a word. Not a single word. The instructor might as well have been speaking German, because I didn't have a clue what he was saying. That lecture made my decision real easy for me. I went back to the dorm and called my parents. I explained to them all the struggles I was having and that I thought I was more suited for business than engineering. Like always, my parents were very supportive and encouraged me to just relax and figure out what I needed to do to get accepted into the K.U. business school.

The K.U. business school was located in Summerfield Hall, not far from Naismith Hall. That would make getting to and from most of my classes over the next few years much easier. I didn't have any trouble getting into the K.U. School of Business. Majoring in business just made a whole lot more sense for me. I was really good at math, and finance came easy for me as well. I enjoyed most of my business classes, and the instructors were great at opening my eyes to many solutions to real-world problems. I feel like I received an excellent education at the University of Kansas.

In my sophomore year at the University of Kansas I went out for the K.U. Wrestling Club. Because I had just switched majors from mechanical engineering to business administration, my class load was extremely light my first semester. That left me with plenty of time to focus on other little hobbies like table tennis and wrestling. There were about ten guys in the K.U. Wrestling Club when I joined it. We were all former high school wrestlers who still had some competitive fire left, and wrestling provided an opportunity for us to try to relive some of our glory days. About half the guys in the K.U. Wrestling Club placed in their particular states in high school, so the level of competition in practice was pretty good.

Wrestling practices were a couple of hours long, three days a week. We met at Robinson Gymnasium on the K.U. campus. It was a nice facility right across the street from Allen Fieldhouse, the historic home of the Kansas Jayhawk basketball team. We held intra-squad matches quite often, which allowed everyone to get into shape fairly quickly and bring their old, rusty wrestling skills back to life. I had gained twenty pounds in the two years since wrestling in high school and came in weighing about 125 pounds. There were three guys on the team who were within ten pounds of my weight class so I had plenty of competition to challenge me.

The coach of the K.U. Wrestling Club was a really cool guy. He made wrestling fun and reminded me a lot of Coach Gensler back in high school. He was very knowledgeable about the sport and ran tough practices like Coach Gensler had. Unfortunately, he didn't have us prepared for one early-season exhibition match that he had scheduled. Of all of my many experiences in competitive sports, our exhibition match with Division II Northeast Missouri State University will forever go down as my wildest, craziest, funniest sports moment ever. It was an adventure I will never forget.

Eight of us piled into a station wagon and headed up to Kirksville, Missouri, for a 7:00 p.m. exhibition wrestling match with Northeast Missouri

State University. This was going to be our first real wrestling match of the new season, and none of us had any idea what we had gotten ourselves into. Many times, it's the element of surprise that leads to some great memories in life. Little did we all know that we were all   sheep being led to the slaughter. I liked our coach, but he had not fully explained to us the situation that we were about to walk into. All eight of us former high school wrestlers had envisioned going up to Kirksville to a little wrestling room and having a few competitive exhibition matches.

When we finally arrived around 6:50 p.m. at the Northeast Missouri State University campus, we soon discovered that we represented the University of Kansas in a much more significant manner than just as a club team. We were deep into the heart of the state of Missouri, and at this time, the Kansas basketball team was one of the best teams in the country. When we walked in with "Kansas" on the front of our shirts, we represented the hated enemy of many in the Missouri-Kansas border war. There must have been a thousand people there for this so-called exhibition match, and many of them didn't seem to like Kansas very much. After going out to see where we would be wrestling and then seeing the big crowd, we all headed back to the locker room. All eight of us simultaneously busted out laughing once we got into the locker room. We were all thinking the same thing: These people think we are legitimate Division I college athletes. I honestly believe that many of the people there to watch thought we represented big time K.U. athletics. We weren't exactly big-time.

Saying we were big time might have been a bit of an exaggeration. We had only three practices prior to going to Kirksville, and we weren't exactly a bunch of highly recruited scholarship athletes. We were just a group of former high school wrestlers looking to have a little fun on a Saturday night.

Coach had driven up separately and arrived in the locker room a couple of minutes after we had. He began filling in all of the details on the lion's den that we were about to walk into. He started by telling two of our guys that they would be wrestling twice because we were a couple of men short of a full roster. He then broke the news to us that college wrestling matches were eight minutes in length compared to just six minutes in high school. In this college match format, the first two periods are three minutes long and then the last period is two minutes. Everyone's mouth dropped at that wonderful disclosure. We would all be lucky if we were in shape to go three minutes, let alone eight. The coach then had some even better news for me. He told me that they didn't have enough wrestlers in my weight class so I would be going up against a guy who weighed 150 pounds, 25 pounds heavier than me. I remember my exact words in disbelief: "You have got to be kidding me." One big key to my success in high school wrestling had been that my upper-body was bigger and stronger than my opponents'. Now that advantage would be completely negated. At that point, I knew it was going to be an interesting night.

A few times arise in life when you know you are dead meat. This was one of those moments for me.

Northeast Missouri State had a real collegiate wrestling program, and when they came out running around in their new purple and white uniforms, I don't believe I was the only one of us wishing I was back in the dorm studying for a calculus test. The crowd standing and cheering for their home team didn't help, either. I just told myself to go down swinging.

The first match of the night gave us one of our best chances of winning. Our 125-pound wrestler had placed sixth in the state of Iowa in high school. He was a talented kid, and if anyone looked like he could make it the full eight minutes, it would be him.

The first period was closely fought, and our 125-pound guy led 4-3. He led until midway through the third period, when the Northeast Missouri State wrestler regained the lead on a single-leg takedown. The guy from Northeast Missouri State then went on to win the match 9-8, eliminating one of our best chances for a victory. By this time, the crowd had really started getting into the exhibition match. My match was next, and as I started out onto the mat, I recall, the crowd became quite a bit quieter. I assumed it was in anticipation of seeing a triple amputee wrestle at the collegiate level. Believe me, I had no idea what to expect either. I did know that I wasn't going to go down without a fight.

One thing I knew for certain: the wrestler I was going up against from Northeast Missouri State was more nervous than I was. I could see it in his face and eyes. He was literally shaking when we shook hands before the start of the match. I looked at it as a no-lose situation. No one in that sports arena expected a triple amputee outweighed by 25 pounds to win. I knew that if I was going to win, I had to catch my opponent in a mistake and make him pay dearly for it. Going up against a heavier wrestler who was as strong as I was would wear me down a lot faster, too. If I was going to win, I had to do it in the first period. After that, I would have nothing left.

The referee blew the whistle, and my opponent came right out after me. I think sometimes being nervous can cause guys to be in a hurry. My opponent shot in on me, and I caught him in a front head-lock. I then tried to roll him to his back, but he rolled right through. I then quickly pushed him away, and we went neutral again. Just a couple of seconds later, my opponent was able to knock me off balance and score the first takedown. At this time, my opponent made a mistake that nearly cost him the match. It was the mistake I had been hoping and waiting for. I don't know if it was because he was in a rush to get the match over with or because he was overconfident, but my opponent sunk in a half nelson without first breaking me down to the mat. It was still early enough in the first period that I still had all of my energy and strength left. I cranked down with every-thing I had on his arm and stepped across his head, putting him onto his back for just a split second. I reached to catch his other arm to put him away but was unable to catch it. My coach and I both would concur later that I was inches away right then from winning my first collegiate match. When I rolled my opponent to his back, I heard a surprised "oooh" from the crowd. I'm not sure they were expecting much from my one-armed, no-legged frame. Sports many times come down to a game of inches, and we've all heard plenty of fish stories about the big ones that got away. Well, I had a 150-pound big one on the hook but couldn't get him into the boat. I have to give my opponent credit: he found a way to escape.

The only good news for me out of my near pin of my opponent was that I scored a point for an escape. We were now in the neutral position, and my opponent was leading 2-1. We went back and forth over the next minute and a half, taking shots at one another without either of us having much success. Then with less than thirty seconds left to go in the first period, my opponent shot in on a double-leg takedown and threw me onto my back. All I can remember is the crowd yelling, screaming, and pounding on their seats, calling for a pin. I recall being on my back, fighting to keep from getting pinned, and looking up just in time to see the most awesome looking scoreboard on the sports arena ceiling that I had ever seen. I thought, *That scoreboard is awesome!* With less than two seconds to go in the first period, the referee pounded the mat, signaling that I had lost by way of pin. I had just lost my first collegiate wrestling match, but all I could think about was how cool their scoreboard looked. Trust me, it was one awesome-looking scoreboard!

Northeast Missouri State University ended up winning eight out of the nine matches against the K.U. Wrestling Club that cool Saturday night in the fall of 1987. We were really fortunate to have found a way to win one. It had turned out to be a trip to Kirksville, Missouri, that none of us former high school wrestlers would ever forget, however. We had been able in one night to not only create a lifetime of memories, but also give the Northeast Missouri State wrestling team a lot of confidence going into their upcoming wrestling season. We let them believe that they could actually beat Kansas!

God Sent You on a Mission

I grew up a big Kansas Jayhawk basketball fan. I'm not embarrassed to admit that that was the number-one reason why I chose to cross over the Missouri-Kansas border and attend the University of Kansas. When I was around 12 years old, a neighborhood friend of mine invited me to go with him to the Big Eight Holiday Tournament at Kemper Arena in Kansas City, Missouri. I had never seen college basketball live before, and after watching K.U. star Darnell Valentine play, I was quickly converted. I would forever be a Jayhawk.

Less than seven years later, I was a freshman at K.U. attending a fraternity party on campus with several friends I had recently met. It was the first week of school and the first official party of my college career. I was just kind of standing around, looking for the right group of people to approach to start a conversation with. To my surprise, K.U.'s current basketball superstar, Danny Manning, went out of his way to walk over and introduce himself to me. I couldn't believe it! Danny Manning was probably the best college basketball player in the country and was not only my hero but also the hero of everyone who followed the game. It's pretty awesome when your heroes turn out to be great guys too. Danny Manning was easily one of the most down-to-earth superstars there's ever been. I remember watching him playing wiffleball games with some of my fellow students and friends in front of Oliver Hall. On several other occasions, Danny Manning went out of his way to say hello to me when I passed him at Naismith Hall and on the K.U. campus. My second year at K.U., I would get the thrill of a lifetime when I was able to cheer Danny Manning and the rest of the Kansas Jayhawk basketball team on to the national title.

After a loss to Kansas State in the 1988 Big Eight Tournament, a trip to the Final Four did not appear to be in the cards for the Kansas Jayhawks. I remember Dad and I leaving Kemper Arena in Kansas City a little discouraged after watching the loss to Mitch Richmond and the Kansas State Wildcats. We were just happy that Kansas had done enough to get into the NCAA basketball tournament. Kansas needed to finish the regular season winning nine out of their last twelve games to end with a 21-11 record. They would enter the 1988 NCAA tournament as a sixth seed in the Midwest Region.

Early-season injuries and some tough losses made Kansas's road to the national championship an amazing story. In 1988, Kansas got off to a disappointing 12-8 start that included 1-4 in the Big Eight Conference. Playing against St. Johns early in the season, they lost starter Archie Marshall to a season-ending knee injury. K.U. lost nine scholarship players to injury, academic problems, or other issues. Coach Larry Brown was entering his fifth season at K.U. and ended up having to recruit two players off the K.U. football team just to fill the roster.

Coach Brown, who had led K.U. to a Final Four appearance in 1986, displayed perhaps the greatest coaching performance of his career in 1988. With all the injury and academic turmoil, Brown had to shift the pieces of the K.U. team all around. He moved Kevin Pritchard into the point guard position. Kevin was normally a shooting guard. Milt Newton replaced Archie Marshall in the starting lineup and played forward. Newton became a big scorer for Kansas and played a key role in the national title run. Coach Brown also moved sophomore guard Jeff Gueldner into the starting lineup. Gueldner's outside shooting really helped spread out opponents' defenses, allowing Danny Manning to be even more productive.

The Jayhawks' road to the Final Four in Kansas City, Missouri, began at the Devaney Center in Lincoln, Nebraska. Their opening-round game would be against the Xavier Musketeers, who came in as the 11th seed in the Midwest region. The Musketeers came in with a 15-game winning streak but were no match for the Jayhawks, who hit their free throws down the stretch and ended up winning 85-72. K.U. was expecting to have to take on the third-seeded N.C. State Wolfpack in the second round: however, the Wolfpack got beat by the 14th-seeded Murray State Racers. That began a streak of upset victories that opened up the door for Kansas. The three top-seeded teams in the Midwest region were upset right before playing the Jayhawks.

It is said that there is usually one game a team has to survive if it is to win the NCAA tournament. The game between Kansas and Murray State proved to be that kind of a game. Murray State missed a short jump shot with one second left, allowing Kansas to escape with a thrilling 61-58 victory. The win would put the Jayhawks back into the Sweet 16 for the third consecutive year.

The Midwest regional would be held in Pontiac, Michigan. The Jayhawks' opponent would be the seventh-seeded Vanderbilt Commodores. The Commodores had just upset the number-two seed Pittsburgh Panthers to get to the Sweet 16 game against Kansas. Danny Manning would have one of his best games in the NCAA tournament against Vanderbilt, scoring 38 points. K.U. won 77-64 and advanced to the Elite 8 against its archrival, the Kansas State Wildcats.

Kansas State was seeded fourth in the Midwest region and had just upset the top-seeded Purdue Boilermakers to get the chance to play Kansas for a trip to the Final Four. In the first half, K.U. did an excellent job defending Kansas State's biggest star, Mitch Richmond, but was unable to stop Will Scott, who scored 13 points and led the Wildcats to a 29-27 halftime lead. The lead would have been larger if not for a last-second three-point shot by K.U. reserve guard Scooter Barry.

Kansas State came out in the second half and increased its lead to 40-35 with just under 16 minutes to play. Kansas had made some defensive adjustments at halftime, however, and were able to stop Will Scott in the second half. With a little under 14 minutes left in regulation, Kansas regained the lead, 43-42, on a steal and dunk by reserve Keith Harris. The Jayhawks then put the game away with a 20-8 run led by Milt Newton, Kevin Pritchard, and Scooter Barry. After knocking down some late free throws, the Jayhawks, who had come into the NCAA tournament unranked, won the game with a final score of 71-58 and were headed back to the Final Four in Kansas City!

The Kansas Jayhawks, 25-11, would face the fifth-ranked Duke Blue Devils, 28-6, in one of the semifinal games of the NCAA Tournament. The winner would play against the winner of the Arizona-Oklahoma semifinal game for the championship. In its prior game Duke had upset the number-one-ranked Temple Owls to make it to Kansas City. Just over a month earlier, Duke had beaten K.U. 74-70 in overtime at Allen Fieldhouse in Lawrence, Kansas. Duke had also beaten Kansas 71-67 two years before in the Final Four. Those two losses provided added incentives for the Jayhawks to find a way to beat Duke. This was the Final Four, though, and both teams had plenty to play for.

Kansas came out on fire and jumped all over Duke 14-0 to begin the game. Any questions about whether the Jayhawks could stay with the Blue Devils were immediately answered. Nine minutes into the game, Kansas had a 24-6 lead.

The Kansas defense was awesome, led by Danny Manning who was making steals and rejecting shots all over the court. Duke scored only two points in its first 11 possessions of the game. Kansas took a large lead into halftime and needed to play just 20 more great minutes of basketball to play for a national title.

Kansas extended its lead to 49-33 early in the second half. Duke then went on a 13-2 run, however, and cut the Kansas lead to just 51-46 with less than ten minutes to play in the game. Both teams had their own little scoring runs over the next six minutes, but Kansas still held a small 55-52 lead with four minutes left. Four minutes doesn't sound like a long time to play, but it seemed like an eternity as Kansas and Duke exchanged baskets. Manning and Pritchard scored buckets for Kansas, and Quin Snyder scored for Duke, making it 59-54 with just over two minutes to go. About this time, K.U. fans could sense that a Jayhawk victory and a trip to the title game were imminent. The crowd at Kemper Arena was decisively in favor of the local underdog Jayhawks and provided a big boost to Kansas. Kansas hit its free throws down the stretch to put the game away 66-59 and advance to the NCAA national championship game against the Oklahoma Sooners.

The Oklahoma Sooners entered the national title game Monday night with a 35-3 record and averaging 103.5 points per game. The Sooners had just beaten the Arizona Wildcats 86-78 in the other semifinal game on Saturday. Few people gave the 26-11 Kansas Jayhawks a chance of winning the game, and many thought that Oklahoma might run Kansas clear off the court. The Sooners were led by three future first-round NBA draft picks in Mookie Blaylock, Stacey

King, and Harvey Grant. To beat Oklahoma, Kansas would have to play a nearly perfect game and do what only three other teams had pulled off all season. It was only the third time in history that two teams from the same conference would play for the title.

Kansas came out and surprised everyone by running with the Sooners right from the start. Most people did not expect the Jayhawks to run with Oklahoma because the Sooners were so explosive on offense. The Jayhawks were able to match offensive punches with Oklahoma through the first twenty minutes, though. Kansas came out and made 17 out of its first 20 shots from the field. The pace of the first half was so fast and frantic that one of the referees looked like he needed an oxygen tank. Oklahoma sharp shooter Dave Sieger hit all six of his three-point shots in the first half, and the Jayhawks shot a combined 71% from the field. The two teams headed to the locker room at the half, tied 50-50.

In the second half, the frantic pace of the game slowed down a little. Kansas continued playing extremely well but fell behind, 65-60, with a little more than 12 minutes to go in the game. The Jayhawks slowly pecked away at the Oklahoma lead and went in front for good on a basket by Kevin Pritchard. The score was 73-71 with just over five and a half minutes left to play. The Jayhawks then began to let the air out of the ball and spread out Oklahoma's defense. With the Oklahoma defense all spread out, the Jayhawks began to cut back door and score some easy baskets. Chris Piper hit a shot that barely beat the shot clock, giving Kansas a 77-71 lead with just over three minutes left. The Jayhawk fans at Kemper Arena could sense that the seemingly impossible dream might be about to come true! Oklahoma hadn't gotten to the championship game by going down easily though. Oklahoma came storming back and closed the deficit to 78-77 with just 41 seconds left. Scooter Barry then went to the free throw line for Kansas and made one of two free throws. When Barry missed the second free throw, Danny Manning grabbed the rebound and was fouled. Manning then hit both free throws giving Kansas an 81-77 lead with 14 seconds to go. Grace scored another basket for Oklahoma, but a couple more free throws from Danny Manning put the game away and gave the Kansas Jayhawks their first national championship in 36 years!

Danny Manning had 31 points, 18 rebounds, and 5 steals in the winning effort. Manning was also voted the NCAA tournament most valuable player. Possibly the biggest story of the game was that K.U.'s supporting cast of Milt Newton, Kevin Pritchard, Chris Piper, and Clint Normore went a combined 19 for 22 shooting. The Jayhawks shot an amazing 63% for the game. Milt Newton was six-for-six with 15 points. Kevin Pritchard was six-for-seven shooting and had 13 points.

As soon as the game was over, my friends and I bolted out of the dorm and dashed up the hill to the K.U. campus to celebrate. It was K.U.'s first national title since 1952, and students were ready to party like there was no tomorrow! People were hanging out of trees, sitting on top of cars, and sitting on each other's shoulders, screaming and shouting that their Jayhawks were number one! It was a night none of us would ever forget. "Danny and the Miracles," as they would later be called, gave us all the thrill of our young lives when they shocked the nation and beat the heavily favored Sooners from Oklahoma!

One day in the spring of 1989, I was sitting out on the beautiful campus at Kansas University when a couple of guys from a Christian campus ministry came up to talk to me. They asked me two simple questions. The first question was "If you were to die today, where would you go?" The follow-up question was "Why do you believe this?" I answered their initial question with the first thing that popped into my head: "I would hope I would go to heaven." I honestly didn't know why I believed that, though. I guess I assumed like most people that I was a good person and good people must go to heaven. Right? I was honestly caught off guard by the two questions, but they made me really think about my life and what I truly believed. I ended up telling the guys what dorm I was staying at and that I would be willing to attend a Bible study sometime.

A couple of weeks later, one of the guys from the Christian campus ministry tracked me down at Naismith Hall. I told him that I did not have a Bible and asked him if he would help me go and pick out a good one, so we went to the local Christian bookstore and I purchased one of the new translations of the Bible (the NIV version). I wanted a version that would be easy for me to understand. We then went back to the dorm and had my first study of the Bible.

I quickly learned from studying the Bible that some of my basic assumptions about who goes to heaven and who doesn't were based on little more than wishful thinking. If I had it my way, everyone would get to go to heaven. Or at least all the good people would go to heaven. But my assumption that there was actually such a thing as a good person was based on what? Where did I get the idea that some people are good? Who said anyone is good? Good compared to whom or what? I usually liked comparing myself to Adolph Hitler. Surely, compared to Hitler, I was a pretty good person. Then I began to read where Jesus said that God alone is good. Now that was a scary thought. God alone is good. Those words made me pause and think. It was at that moment that I started to realize that the bar representing the definition of good was set a lot higher than Adolph Hitler; it was actually God Himself. God was the standard of good. Wow! I have to admit, that was a little terrifying to see. Seeing that changed the whole game for me. How could I ever be as good as God is? The answer is, I couldn't. That's why the Bible says I need a savior. That is why God sent Jesus Christ into the world to die on the cross for my sins. I'm not good enough to go to heaven, but the savior is! He can carry me into heaven on His back!

I can remember one night that same week, bowing my head and saying a prayer similar to this: "Lord Jesus Christ, Son of God, have mercy on me, a sinner. God, I know that You love me, and I believe that You sent Christ to die on the cross for me. I receive You into my heart as my Lord and Savior. In Jesus' name I pray. Amen." After that moment, my life was never the same. I was born again.

John 3:1-15 says, "Now there was a man of the Pharisees named Nicodemus, a member of the Jewish ruling council. He came to Jesus at night and said, 'Rabbi, we know you are a teacher who has come from God. For no one could perform the miraculous signs you are doing if God were not with him.'

"In reply Jesus declared, 'I tell you the truth, no one can see the kingdom of God unless he is born again.'

"'How can a man be born when he is old?' Nicodemus asked. 'Surely he cannot enter a second time into his mother's womb to be born!'

"Jesus answered, 'I tell you the truth, no one can enter the kingdom of God unless he is born of water and the Spirit. Flesh gives birth to flesh, but the Spirit gives birth to spirit. You should not be surprised at my saying, "You must be born again." The wind blows wherever it pleases. You hear its sound, but you cannot tell where it comes from or where it is going. So it is with everyone born of the Spirit.'

"'How can this be?' Nicodemus asked.

"'You are Israel's teacher,' said Jesus, 'and you do not understand these things? I tell you the truth, we speak of what we know, and we testify to what we have seen, but still you people do not accept our testimony. I have spoken to you of earthly things and you do not believe; how then will you believe if I speak of heavenly things? No one has ever gone into heaven except the one who came from heaven, the

Son of Man. Just as Moses lifted up the snake in the desert, so the Son of Man must be lifted up, that everyone who believes in him may have eternal life."

We here the term "born again" but what exactly does it mean? When Jesus explained to Nicodemus, he made a comparison to the wind. There's a mystery to it. He indicated that being born again is a work of the Spirit. I know this about my rebirth: Before I was born again, I knew about God. God was some impersonal, all-powerful being somewhere out there who had created everything for some unknown purpose. After being born again, I knew God in a personal way and knew that He had a purpose for my existence. God became my friend, and a relationship began. In John 17:3, Jesus says, "Now this is eternal life: that they may know you, the only true God, and Jesus Christ, whom you have sent."

Why did Jesus say that we must be born again? According to the Bible, the first time we are all born into this world, we are born dead~not physically, but spiritually. Our spirits are separated from God's spirit because of sin and need to be reconnected. At the cross of Christ, God built a bridge between Himself and sinful men. When we believe in Jesus Christ, we walk across that bridge into the arms of our Heavenly Father and our spirits are reconnected to God.

Our missions in life begin when we are born again. God has sent you into this world on a mission that is exciting, is fulfilling, and has eternal signifi-
The mission that God has given to you gives meaning. Just as Jesus was sent on a mission, I have been sent on missions. Jesus fully

understood that He had been sent on a mission from the Father. At the age of 12, Jesus said in Luke 2:49, "I must be about my Father's business." At the end of His mission, Jesus said from the cross (John 19:30), "It is finished." When you fulfill your mission, you bring glory to God, but doing so may cause you not to achieve all of your personal goals and ambitions in life. Jesus clearly told people to count the cost. Living a life full of meaning and significance does not come without a price.

One great example of a man who knew and understood that God had sent him on a mission was Dr. Martin Luther King Jr. Martin Luther King Jr. was born on January 15, 1929, in Atlanta, Georgia. His name was originally Michael King Jr., but after a family trip to Germany in 1934, his father changed both of their names to Martin Luther after the Protestant leader Martin Luther. Martin Luther King Jr. was quite the scholar and was able to skip both the ninth and twelfth grades. He entered Morehouse College at the young age of 15 and graduated in 1948 with a Bachelor of Arts degree in sociology. He then went on to Crozer Theological Seminary in Chester, Pennsylvania, and graduated in 1951 with a Bachelor of Divinity degree. When he was just 25 years old, in 1954, King became the pastor of the Dexter Avenue Baptist Church in Montgomery, Alabama. On June 5, 1955, he received his Doctor of Philosophy from Boston University.

Martin Luther King Jr. was born at God's perfect time to fulfill God's appointed mission. King quickly became a great leader in the civil rights movement for black Americans. In 1955, he led the Montgomery Bus Boycott after Rosa Parks was arrested for refusing to give up her seat. The Montgomery Bus Boycott lasted for 385 days and resulted in King's house being bombed. The boycott continued right up to a United States District Court ruling in the case of Browder v. Gayle, which brought an end to racial segregation on all public buses in Montgomery, Alabama.

A man who was a huge influence on Martin Luther King Jr. was civil rights leader Howard Thurman. Howard Thurman had been a classmate of King's father at Morehouse College and had himself been greatly influenced by Mahatma Gandhi of India. Thurman had taught King about Gandhi and his method of nonviolent resistance against British colonial rule in India during the first half of the 20th century. King went and visited Gandhi's birthplace in India in 1959. After his trip to India, King was certain that nonviolent resistance was the best weapon for African-Americans to use in their struggle for civil rights.

In 1957, Martin Luther King Jr., along with other civil rights activists, founded the Southern Christian Leadership Conference. They created the group to organize the power of black churches to carry out nonviolent protests in their struggle for civil rights. Martin Luther King Jr. served as the first president of the Southern Christian Leadership Conference and continued to do so until his death on April 4, 1968. As the leader of the SCLC, King led a group who organized the March on Washington for

Jobs and Freedom on August 28, 1963. The g
sought to bring about many social and economic
changes with the march, such as a $2 minimum wage,
significant civil rights legislation, an end to racial segregation in public schools, and a law to prohibit racial
discrimination in employment. More than a quarter
of a million people attended the march that culmi-
nated with King giving one of the great speeches in
American history: "I Have a Dream." King went on
to lead nonviolent protests and marches that eventually resulted in the passing of the Civil Rights Act of
1964 and the 1965 Voting Rights Act. It is scary to
think about, but I am fully convinced that if it were
not for great men like Martin Luther King Jr., we
would still be living in a society with segregated public restrooms. I am thankful and glad that God sent
King on a mission!

The night before he was assassinated, April 3,
1968, Dr. Martin Luther King Jr. gave what would
turn out to be his last sermon at the Mason Temple in
Memphis, Tennessee. The title of the sermon was "I
See the Promised Land." The last part of King's sermon reads, "Well I don't know what will happen now.
We've got some difficult days ahead. But it doesn't
matter with me now. Because I've been to the mountaintop. And I don't mind. Like anybody, I would
like to live a long life. Longevity has its place. But
I'm not concerned about that now. I just want to do
God's will. And He's allowed me to go up to the
mountain. And I've looked over. And I've seen the
promised land. I may not get there with you. But I
want you to know tonight, that we, as a people will

get to the promised land. And I'm happy tonight. I'm not worried about anything. I'm not fearing any man. Mine eyes have seen the glory of the coming of the Lord."

I was just over a month past my thirteenth birthday when I heard the news that President Ronald Reagan had been shot. I could not believe my ears at the time. It shakes your world when an assassin takes aim at the leader of the free world. On March 30, 1981, John Hinckley, an unstable man seeking the affection of actress Jodi Foster, had shot President Reagan as the president was leaving the Washington Hilton. It was only two months into the president's first term and was nearly the shortest presidency in American history.

After the events of that day had been examined, Reagan's miraculous survival appeared to have been nothing short of divine providence. To begin with, the quick thinking and diagnosis by Secret Service Agent Jerry Parr was the first of several fortunate events that saved Reagan's life that terrifying day. Jerry Parr recognized immediately that Reagan had been hit and told the driver to get to the hospital immediately. Once arriving at George Washington University Hospital Reagan's amazing good fortune continued. Two of the university's chief surgeons were both conveniently right there that day to take care of the president. The prompt medical attention that Reagan received not only helped save his life, but also allowed him to quickly recover. If that weren't enough to convince one of God's intervention, Hinckley's inability to directly hit his target should put any doubts to rest. Hinckley fired a .22 caliber revolver six times in three seconds and managed to miss the president with all but the final bullet. The first shot hit White House Press Secretary James Brady in the head. The second hit District of Columbia police officer Thomas Delahanty in the back. The third bullet hit a window in a building across the street. The fourth shot hit Secret Service agent Timothy McCarthy in the stomach. The fifth shot hit the bulletproof glass window of the president's limousine. The bullets Hinckley used during the assassination attempt were designed to explode in the body. That day, the sixth bullet that hit the president bounced off the armored car, hit one of Reagan's ribs, went through a lung, and finally stopped less than an inch from his heart. It apparently wasn't Reagan's day to die.

Reagan himself would later say that he was sure that God had spared him. He vowed that whatever time he had left was for God. Speaking about Reagan surviving this assassination attempt, Mother Teresa would later tell him, "There is a purpose to this. This has happened to you at this time because your country and the world need you."

Reagan clearly believed that God had a mission and a destiny for everyone. He displayed this belief in a letter he wrote to a woman who had written him regarding her handicapped son. Reagan wrote, "I find myself believing very deeply that God has a plan for each one of us. Some with little faith and even less testing seem to miss in their mission, or else we perhaps fail to see their imprint on the lives of others. But bearing what we cannot change and going on with what God has given us, confident there is a destiny, somehow seems to bring a reward we wouldn't exchange for any other. It takes a lot of fire and heat to make a piece of steel."

Ronald Reagan's mission in life had begun at an early age. After reading Harold Bell Wright's book, *That Printer of Udell's*, Reagan converted to Christianity and was baptized at the age of 11. He went onto embrace a model of "practical Christianity" that would end up having a huge impact on the world stage. God sent Ronald Reagan on a mission to Moscow!

In October 1917, the Bolshevik (Communist) party, led by Vladimir Lenin began a revolution in Russia that eventually led to the Union of Soviet Socialist Republics (USSR). Lenin was an atheist and a disciple of Karl Marx. Lenin gave up on God as a teenager and his rejection of God naturally drew him to Marx's ideas. Marx was famous for saying that religion was the opiate of the people. Marx dreamed of a utopian classless society where crime would become unnecessary and disappear. In his dream vision for the world, there would be an international socialist brotherhood where everyone would have their equal portion and where there would be no more wars. Marx believed that the only way his perfect world could be realized was by destroying the church. Lenin agreed and professed, "Religion is the biggest lie, that humanity has ever invented." The Bolsheviks, under Lenin's leadership, declared war on God and any demonstration of religious faith. They began an all-out assault on religious freedom that continued for decades until the late 1980s.

A man who had a major influence on Ronald Reagan and his view of Soviet communism was Whittaker Chambers. Whittaker Chambers was born on April 1, 1901, in Philadelphia, Pennsylvania. He joined the Communist Party of the United States in 1924 and from 1932 to 1938 spied for the Soviet KGB. He later rejected communism and converted to Christianity. In his memoir, *Witness*, published in 1952, Chambers describes in detail his road from communism to Christianity. He says that ultimately, his renunciation of communism came down to its faith in man and rejection of God. Chambers said the problem with communism was not its economics but its atheism. He wrote, "The Communist vision is the vision of Man without God."

Reagan was deeply moved by Chambers' book and quoted from it throughout his public life. One of many problems that Reagan saw with communism was its denial of the importance of the individual. To Reagan, the individual was infinitely more important than the state. It was intolerable to Reagan that the state could deny individuals their opportunity to hear the message of salvation. For Reagan, the eternal salvation of millions of people in the communist countries was at stake. On December 9, 1983, Reagan revealed the true motive of his heart when he said, "In many countries people aren't even allowed to read the Bible. It is up to us to make sure the message of hope and salvation gets through."

When Reagan became president in January 1981, he believed it was America's responsibility to combat atheistic Soviet communism. Reagan saw his presidency in part as an opportunity to be a missionary and to free those trapped by communism. Reagan's plans to defeat communism had started well before he became president, however. In 1977, Reagan had told Richard Allen, his foreign policy adviser, his strategy toward the USSR: "It is this: we win and they lose."

Another part of God's mission for Ronald Reagan appears to have been for Reagan to play a key role in ending the Cold War and defeating communism. On June 12, 1987, President Ronald Reagan gave a speech to the people of West Berlin, challenging Soviet leader Mikhail Gorbachev's commitment to increasing freedom in the Eastern Bloc Reagan would proclaim in one of his most famous speeches, "General Secretary Gorbachev, if you seek peace, if you seek prosperity for the Soviet Union and Eastern Europe, if you seek liberalization: Come here to this gate! Mr. Gorbachev, open this gate! Mr. Gorbachev, tear down this wall!" The wall he was speaking of was the Berlin Wall, a twelve-foot concrete wall that extended for a hundred miles around West Berlin. The wall had been built by the Communists in August 1961 to keep Germans from leaving Communist-run East Berlin into Democratic West Berlin. The wall had grown to symbolize the Cold War between the United States and the USSR.

On May 29, 1988, Reagan traveled to Moscow for a fourth summit meeting with Soviet leader Mikhail Gorbachev. President Reagan desperately wanted to see religious freedom brought back to t₁ Soviet Union. More specifically, he wanted to see Christianity in Moscow. Reagan believed that the Soviet people's hunger for religion would play a critical role in bringing about change in the USSR. He made it a point to promote biblical Christianity, believing that the message and the word of God could reach deep into people's hearts and bring about change.

Mikhail Gorbachev was the first Soviet leader to make any effort at reform by introducing the concept known as glasnost, which meant "political openness." Though Gorbachev may not have believed in God, there were signs that he may have believed in a higher power. He was clearly the only Soviet leader who wasn't hostile to religion, and he brought about an end to decades of religious persecution. Reagan kept pressuring Gorbachev for more reform, believing that more needed to be done. In the late 1980s, religious freedoms were restored in the USSR, and a religious revival broke out. The Orthodox Church opened thousands of parishes all across Russia, enjoying freedoms that weren't seen even in America. Toward the end of his God-given mission, Reagan declared, "Freedom is the universal right of all of God's children. The cause of freedom is the cause of God. I believe God intended for us to be free."

Another man in history who knew that God had sent him on a mission was Saul of Tarsus, who would later become the Apostle Paul. Saul was a citizen of Rome and a member of the Jewish religious sect known as the Pharisees. Saul was fiercely opposed to Christianity and a persecutor of early Christians. In Galatians 1:13-14, Paul describes his pre-conversion life: "For you have heard of my previous way of life in Judaism, how intensely I persecuted the church of God and tried to destroy it. I was advancing in Judaism beyond many Jews of my own age and was extremely zealous for the traditions of my fathers."

So what exactly happened to Saul from Tarsus that caused him to become Paul the Apostle? He met Jesus Christ on the road to Damascus while traveling to persecute Christians, and the encounter changed his life forever. Saul was born again and was transformed into the apostle Paul. In one of the great ironies in human history, the biggest opponent of Christianity became its greatest proponent. God had a special mission for Paul to fulfill. He was to be the "Apostle to the Gentiles." Acts 9:15 says, "But the Lord said to Ananias, 'Go! This man is my chosen instrument to carry my name before the Gentiles and their kings and before the people of Israel.'" (From the Jewish perspective, if you were not a Jew, you were a Gentile.) Paul set out on his God-given mission with a passion and changed the course of the world's history. Thirteen letters in the New Testament are credited to Paul and his writings have influenced Church doctrine more than any other New Testament author.

Paul compared our mission in life to running a race. The Corinthians, to whom Paul wrote, were familiar with the foot races in their own Isthmian games, which were held every other year. In 1

Corinthians 9:24-25, Paul writes, "Do you not know that in a race all the runners run, but only one gets the prize? Run in such a way as to get the prize. Everyone who competes in the games goes into strict training. They do it to get a crown that will not last; but we do it to get a crown that will last forever." Near the end of his mission, Paul declares in 2 Timothy 4:7, "I have fought the good fight, I have finished the race, I have kept the faith."

My favorite hymn is the "Battle Hymn of the Republic." What I love about the hymn is its awesome and powerful words. The words of that awe-inspiring hymn were written during the American civil war by a lady named Julia W. Howe. In 1861, Howe was visiting a Union Army camp and overheard some soldiers singing the song "John Brown's Body." At that time, America had no official national hymn. Howe wrote a new set of lyrics in a poem titled "The Battle Hymn of the Republic," which was published in *The Atlantic Monthly* in 1862. Her poem put to the music for "John Brown's Body" came to be what we know today as "The Battle Hymn of the Republic." The hymn has been played at the funerals of American president Ronald Reagan and American senator Robert Kennedy. The hymn has also found its way into the hearts of millions of people all over the world. All the words of that hymn give me the chills, but the verse that grabs me and moves me to action says, "As He died to make men holy, let us live to make men free." I want that to be my personal battle hymn for the rest of my life. I want all men to know the God who set me

...e. I want everyone to know that their sins can be forgiven and they can have eternal life through faith in Jesus Christ. His truth really is marching on!

1. Mine eyes have seen the glory of the coming of the Lord;
   He is trampling out the vintage where the grapes of wrath are stored;
   He hath loosed the fateful lightning of His terrible swift sword;
   His truth is marching on.
   Glory! Glory! Hallelujah! Glory! Glory! Hallelujah!
   Glory! Glory! Hallelujah! His truth is marching on.

2. I have seen Him in the watch fires of a hundred circling camps
   They have builded Him an altar in the evening dews and damps;
   I can read His righteous sentence by the dim and flaring lamps;
   His day is marching on.
   Glory! Glory! Hallelujah! Glory! Glory! Hallelujah!
   Glory! Glory! Hallelujah! His day is marching on.

3. I have read a fiery Gospel writ in burnished rows of steel
   "As ye deal with My contemners, so with you My grace shall deal";
   Let the Hero, born of woman, crush the serpent with His heel,
   Since God is marching on.
   Glory! Glory! Hallelujah! Glory! Glory! Hallelujah!
   Glory! Glory! Hallelujah! Since God is marching on.

4. He has sounded forth the trumpet that shall never call retreat;
   He is sifting out the hearts of men before His judgment seat;
   Oh, be swift, my soul, to answer Him! Be jubilant, my feet;
   Our God is marching on.
   Glory! Glory! Hallelujah! Glory! Glory! Hallelujah!
   Glory! Glory! Hallelujah! Our God is marching on.

5. In the beauty of the lilies Christ was born across the sea,
With a glory in His bosom that transfigures you and me:
As He died to make men holy, let us live to make men
free;
While God is marching on.
Glory! Glory! Hallelujah! Glory! Glory! Hallelujah!
Glory! Glory! Hallelujah! While God is marching on.

6. He is coming like the glory of the morning on the wave:
He is wisdom to the mighty, He is honor to the brave;
So the world shall be His footstool, and the soul of wrong
His slave:
Our God is marching on.
Glory! Glory! Hallelujah! Glory! Glory! Hallelujah!
Glory! Glory! Hallelujah! Our God is marching on.

At Shriners Hospital in St. Louis, Missouri at the age of one.

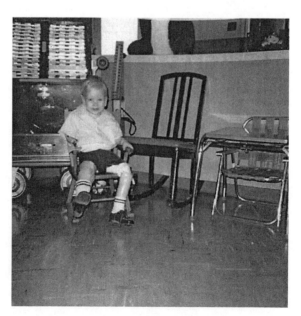

Here I am wearing the artificial arm that I never liked.

The Clark family in front of the vacation guesthouse
in Park Rapids, Minnesota.

The beginning of my swimming career.

Playing ball in back of our house.

Dad, teaching me how to mow the grass.

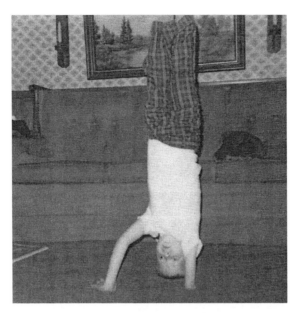

Testing my endurance to see how long I could stand on my head.

My sister, Rhonda, and me playing in the snow.

My best friend, Shaggy, and me.

All four of us kids on Easter 1972.

Dan, Rhonda, and I, surprising mom by
helping out with the dishes.

Dan and I as the two-headed monster on Halloween.

Mom, Dad, and I vacationing in Canada in 1980.

'Captain of the Ship' on Table Rock Lake, Branson, MO.

Here I am with my nephews, Quincy and Michael.

Wrestling victory at Truman High School.

Tim Clark

High School Graduation picture.

CHAPTER 5

Never Give up

Probably, nothing is more common in life than talented, gifted, brilliant people not succeeding and fulfilling their destinies in life. The missing ingredient is usually a mindset that says, "No matter what it takes, I will never give up." That old saying that winners never quit and quitters never win is one of the most important lessons to learn in life. You have to be a person who says, "No matter what it takes, I am going to win the game of life." Life is far too important, and quitting can never be an option.

One of the greatest examples in history of persevering and having a never-give-up attitude was demonstrated in the life of the 16th President of the United States of America, Abraham Lincoln. Lincoln led our country through one of its most difficult periods: the ending of slavery and the resulting civil war. But what preceded the great man we read about in the history books during the civil war period, 1861-1865, was a life filled with challenges, disappointments, and failures. Granted, Lincoln had his share of successes along the way, but if there ever was a figure in American

ho exemplified and lived out the principle of
ing up, it was Abraham Lincoln.

Abraham Lincoln was born February 12, 1809,
near Hodgenville, Hardin County, Kentucky, son of
Thomas and Nancy Hanks Lincoln. Hardship
started early in young Abe's life as his mother died of
"the milk sickness" on October 5, 1818, when he was
only nine years old. On January 20, 1828, his older
sister, Sarah, died in childbirth. On August 6, 1832,
Lincoln was defeated in his bid to be elected to the
Illinois state legislature. In 1833, he failed in business. In 1835, his sweetheart died. In 1836, he had a
nervous breakdown. In 1838, he was defeated for the
position of Illinois House speaker. In 1843, Lincoln
was defeated for nomination for Congress. In 1846,
he was elected to Congress, but in 1848, he lost his
bid to be renominated. In 1849, he was rejected for
the position of land officer. In 1850, his second son,
Eddie, died from tuberculosis. In 1854, Lincoln was
defeated for U.S. Senate. In 1856, he was defeated in
his nomination for Vice President of the United
States. In 1858, he was once again defeated for U.S.
Senate. Then on November 6, 1860, Abraham Lincoln was elected the 16th President of the United
States of America. Wow! At least he kept failing
while attempting to get higher and higher jobs.

One of the things that stood out to me about Abraham Lincoln was his character. Not only did the man
never give up, but he stood up for what he believed and
did not waver under pressure. Jesus said in Luke 6:27,
"But I tell you who hear me: Love your enemies, do
good to those who hate you, bless those who curse

you." Abraham Lincoln gave us a beautiful illustration of this principle in his dealings with one of his biggest political enemies, Edwin Stanton. Edwin Stanton, a Democrat, was one of Lincoln's biggest political enemies and critics. When Lincoln was nominated by the new Republican Party and elected President of the United States, Stanton called him a "low, cunning clown." He criticized Lincoln's physical appearance and compared the new president to primates, but in 1862, when the all-important cabinet position for Secretary of War came open, whom do you think Lincoln appointed to the post? You guessed it: Edwin Stanton. Everyone tried to remind Lincoln just whom he was appointing to his cabinet. They reminded him of how hateful and what a huge enemy Stanton had been. "How could you name such a man?" they asked. Lincoln responded, "He's the most qualified man for the job." Then Lincoln said one of the most powerful statements he ever uttered: "Do we not destroy our enemies when we make them our friends?" In that moment, Lincoln gave us one of the most awesome demonstrations in history of loving our enemies. We always talk and hear about athletes playing on another level, but Lincoln did it on the biggest stage of all, the game of life. Had Lincoln hated Stanton for how Stanton had treated him, they both would have gone to their graves as bitter enemies. Instead, not only did Stanton turn out to be a superb appointment to Secretary of War, but his opinion of Lincoln radically changed as well. After Lincoln's death, Stanton proclaimed, on April 14, 1865, that Lincoln was a great man: "Now he belongs to the ages."

I've had my share of failures and disappointments in sports as well as in life. During those moments, it was hard to see how I would ever find the courage to get up and come back, but as I look back, I believe that failure is just part of the process on the road to success. I have usually learned a whole lot more from my losses than from my victories. The secret is in not ever giving up.

In 1995, I played in the finals for the Standing Disabled Doubles Table Tennis National Championship in Las Vegas, Nevada. My partner and I had just met in Las Vegas and had chosen to play with each other right before the tournament began. We had seen each other play and both knew that we had a chance to do some big things together if we played well. The final would match us up against none other than Tahl Leibovitz of New York. Tahl was an up-and-coming star in United States table tennis. Tahl's eventual ranking would rise into the top 20 in the United States even among able-bodied players. He was a big-time player. Tahl would later go on to win the 2008 U.S. Collegiate National Championship in table tennis and would win many gold medals for the United States in the Paralympics.

Of the four of us players in the final, I was clearly the most disabled. At least according to my dad and me. When you're missing three limbs like I am, it's easy for everyone to see what is wrong with you. There are quite of few other disabilities out there that are quite a bit harder to detect. But I don't believe in complaining or whining about things in life that you have no control over. At least not complaining for very long. I believe in stating your case and then moving on. So I voiced a complaint to the Paralympic Committee people that I believed it to be a little unfair that a triple amputee had to compete against players with disabilities that were much harder to detect. My partner's disability was that his right leg was longer than his left. This caused him to walk with a limp. The rest of his body worked really well, which was fine with me seeing that he was on my team. Tahl's disability was that he had benign tumors in his body. His partner was missing his left leg below the knee: that was the extent of his disabilities. I was relieved to see that at least one other guy was missing a limb besides me, even if it was just one.

My partner and I got together a few minutes before the final match to discuss strategy and try to figure out how we could pull off the biggest upset of our lives. I was a relatively inexperienced table tennis player at that time and certainly had no experience at playing for a national championship. He warned me that Tahl was an incredible offensive player and that I should serve extremely short as to keep Tahl from attacking. Tahl's partner was also an offensive player with very few weaknesses to expose. My game is in blocking and counterattacking. I rarely initiate the offense. It's just not my strength. My partner had a very good offensive game, so we complemented each other very well.

The match began, and to our surprise, we not only were competitive but won game one fairly easily, 21-15. My short serves were working and keeping our opponents out of their offensive game. They both started off cold and missed a lot of easy shots that they would normally hit. It would not have bothered me at all if they would have stayed cold for just one more game and allowed us to sneak off with the title. The bad news was that we had to win two out of three games to 21 to win the match. Our opponents were experienced players and understood that full well. They weren't at all worried, yet.

In the next game, Tahl and his partner turned up the intensity. Trying to block Tahl's topspin loops was extremely challenging. Just the slightest error of angling the paddle would be the difference between hitting a winning shot and having the ball sail four feet off the end of the table. My partner kept us in the second game, however, with some great offensive loops of his own. We both played pretty solidly but ended up losing game two 21-16.

So, it would all come down to the third game for the national title. Now that they had evened up the game count at 1-1, Tahl and his partner's confidence rose immensely. We knew we were going to have to do something extraordinary in the final game. Our opponents had way too much experience at winning close big games to just give it to us. I hoped that their apparent overconfidence would allow us to sneak in and steal the match.

To everyone's amazement, we were able to jump out to an 18-11 lead in the third game. We just needed three more points for the title and a lifetime of celebrating. Surely we could get three more points. All I remember is Tahl Leibovitz telling his partner that he was not going to miss another shot. To my memory, I don't believe he did. Unfortunately, I got a chance to experience firsthand why Tahl Leibovitz would later be ranked in the top 20 U.S. table tennis players. They outscored us 11 to 2 and won 22-20. Losing anything when you're that close is painful, but losing a national title by blowing such a huge lead is a bitter pill to swallow. It's at moments like those that some people wonder why they ever took up the sport to begin with. Three more points, and this story would have ended up in Chapter 7, "Do You Believe in Miracles?" Instead, it ended up here in Chapter 5! As time goes by, however, and you look back and reflect, you begin to see that it's really moments like those that prepare you for even greater and more important victories in the future.

A few years later, in 1999, I would get another big opportunity when I traveled to Las Vegas for the U.S. Standing Disabled National Table Tennis Championships yet again. Things were going well until I ran into former professional baseball and football player Norman Bass. I honestly didn't know who Norman Bass was at the time but would later read about what an amazing athlete he had been in his youth before rheumatoid arthritis had set in.

Norman Bass had pitched for the Kansas City Athletics in the early 1960s. Then at the early age of 25, arthritis had brought an early end to his career. Norman could throw a fastball over 100 mph in his prime. In his rookie season with the Kansas City A's in 1961, Norman earned a spot in baseball's hall of fame by giving up home run number 27 to Roger

Maris in Maris's record-breaking 61 home run season. A couple of years later, after being forced to retire from baseball, Norman had tried out for and made the Denver Broncos as a defensive back. He had played one AFL game as the first black professional athlete to play two big-league sports. After retiring as a professional athlete and then retiring from McDonnell Douglas as a supervisor in 1994, Norman had begun to focus his attention on the sport of table tennis.

Not knowing who Norman Bass was when I played him probably worked to my advantage because we sometimes have a tendency to give guys like that too much respect and admiration based on their past fame and success. But we weren't playing baseball or football. This was table tennis. Ping-Pong. To me, he looked like a guy in his early 60s I should beat. I really expected to beat him, and after winning game one 21-15, it looked like I might be right. Norman Bass was a tough defensive player, though. Facing him was kind of like playing against a wall. I had to be extremely patient and hit through the wall. I had to get four or five high-quality shots on the table to win a point. I'm sure when he looked at me, a triple amputee, he had probably expected to win too.

In the second game, Norman came alive and jumped off to a 15-12 lead. I then scored 8 out of the next 11 points and took a 20-18 lead. That is where I lost patience and blew the match. I remember trying to put him away with two offensive shots that just missed the table. Norman ended up winning the last four points to win game two 22-20. At that point I was mentally in trouble and getting physically tired. I probably wasn't in as good a physical condition as I should have been in. You never think you're going to get tired playing Ping-Pong until you play a guy like Norman Bass. Then you wish you would have spent a few more hours in the gym and done some more rigorous training.

In the third game, I got very fatigued, lost patience, and ultimately lost 21-17. I lost the match two games to one. It was another heartbreaking loss on a pretty big stage. It was another tough pill to swallow. I voiced another small complaint to the Paralympic Committee people about a triple amputee playing against a former two-sport professional athlete with arthritis. But like I said before, life is not always fair, and when we look back at losses like that, they can teach us big lessons if we don't ever give up. Norman Bass went on to represent the United States in the 2000 Paralympic Games in Sydney, Australia.

It was the fall of the year 2000. I was looking for my jacket so I could go home from a long day at work. I always kept my jacket on a hanger in my cubicle at work so I wouldn't lose it and could easily grab it to go home at night. I started asking around to some of my coworkers if they had seen it. Of course, they hadn't. My patience was running a little thin, so finding my jacket was all I could focus on. Finally, I heard one of my coworkers, Cynthia Nguyen, giggling in her cubicle. I quickly suspected that someone might be playing a little trick and hiding my jacket. I went over and asked her, "Do you know where my jacket is?"

Cynthia, a newly hired employee said, "Well, maybe."

I replied, "What do you mean by maybe?"

"Maybe not," She responded and laughed.

I have to be honest, by this time, I normally would have started to get really frustrated and upset. But this girl who I suspected was hiding my jacket was good-looking. I mean on a scale from one to ten, she was at least a nine. "Well, what do you think happened to my jacket?" I asked.

"Maybe somebody stole it," Cynthia replied.

"When could they have stolen my jacket? I've been at my desk all day," I argued in a friendly manner.

"Well if you'd been at your desk all day, your jacket wouldn't be missing," she said, laughing.

"Okay, I'm going home. If you see my jacket, could you please bring it to me? Thank you. See you tomorrow," I said as I walked out the door. The biggest concern for me was that it was my favorite jacket. My mom had just bought it for me as a birthday gift. I firmly believed as I walked out the door that night that Cynthia was playing a game with me and had hidden my jacket. I didn't know exactly why she would have but I was hoping I would just come back the next day and my jacket would mysteriously have reappeared.

Sure enough, I came back to work the next day and my jacket was sitting in my chair. There was also a handwritten note on my jacket. The note said, "I stole your jacket but it was the wrong size so I brought it back. Ha." The note had two initials on it:

CN. Cynthia Nguyen had been playing a game with me. I had been right. She was the new girl in our department. I call her a girl even though she was a 30-year-old woman. As far as I was concerned, she could steal anything she wanted of mine. She was extremely good-looking. Not that guys usually notice things like that, but Cynthia was striking. She was very funny too. We hit it off right from the beginning. It wasn't long after we met that I worked up enough courage to ask her out to dinner and to a movie. Cynthia was Vietnamese and was from a big family of ten kids. She had been married once before and had three kids: Vincent, who was six, Vivian, who was four, and little Valine, who had just turned two.

Cynthia was a big fan of scary movies so when I asked her to pick out the first movie we would ever see together, her selection should not have surprised me. She picked out *Dracula 2000*. Not exactly my first choice of movies, but at that time I honestly would have gone with Cynthia to see just about anything. I was just excited about my new relationship. Where we went or what we saw together really didn't matter to me. So we got to the movie theater and it was packed. This was a relatively new release, and apparently, a few other people out there besides Cynthia liked getting scared. About a third of the way into the movie, Dracula surprisingly jumps out on the screen. That in and of itself was enough to make my heart skip a beat, but Cynthia let out this loud scream in the middle of the theater. I wanted to just crawl under one of the seats and hide after everyone turned around to look at us. We just laughed and shrugged our shoulders as if to say sorry, couldn't help it. And in Cynthia's case, she honestly couldn't. She was a little embarrassed, but it was a memorable moment we would laugh about for years.

This was an exciting period for me. I was really enjoying the time I was spending with my newfound girlfriend. I think we drew a little bit more attention in the workplace than your average couple, though. I believe in a sense, we became kind of like the latest *National Enquirer* headline or *People* magazine story. I believe I knew what everybody was thinking: How could a beautiful woman like Cynthia go out with a disabled guy like him? I wondered the same thing. One of my good friends just came right out and asked the forbidden question, "What in the world is she doing with you?" I knew he was just playing around. I tried to play it dumb and cool and simply threw it back at him: "Can you blame her?" I wasn't going to let any of that bother me. I was way too happy. I think the bottom line was that Cynthia was different. She really was. I was honestly surprised that my disability didn't seem to bother her either. I think that some of the reason for that simply may have been a difference in cultures. I believe that in many of the Asian cultures, they look at disabled people differently. I think they recognize that disabled people are different but that they many times have special gifts from God. Cynthia seemed to be as fascinated by the things I could do as she was by the few things that I couldn't. I recall her telling me that she was amazed that I could type forty words per minute with only one hand and do my job as easily as I could. She was amazed at how easily I drove a car and played sports so well. She was different, and in a good way. She also didn't seem like she had any idea how pretty she was.

After we had gone out together for a couple of months, it came time to finally meet each other's families. To say the least, I was a little apprehensive about meeting Cynthia's family. To say that I was different would be the understatement of the century. I really did not know what to expect from our initial encounter. Cynthia called her sister Skye. We were going to meet Skye and her husband, Louis, at their house that evening. Skye and Louis lived in Overland Park, Kansas, and had been married for a couple of years. It was in November and a little cold outside, so I had my fall jacket with me. I was so worried about how they might react to someone different like me that I put my jacket over my right shoulder to cover my right arm. I guess I was thinking that I would shock them slowly. As it turned out, my worries were way overblown. Cynthia's sister and brother-in-law were extremely nice and friendly. They were both very successful business people as well. They made me feel right at home and normal from the time I first walked in the door. We weren't able to stay very long because Cynthia had to pick up her three kids from her mom's house in Overland Park. (Cynthia's parents helped her out a lot by watching her children.) So we said good-bye to Skye and Louis, and I went out to the car feeling like we had made it through one major hurdle.

I had an opportunity to meet the rest of Cynthia's family the following weekend at her brother Phillip's house. One thing to admire about Cynthia's family is how close they all are. They would get together at each other's houses at least once a week and sometimes more. I was nervous again just like I had been when meeting Skye and Louis. Cynthia's family was great, though. They all treated me just like anyone else and were very friendly. Her parents both came over and greeted me with a big smile and a handshake. I will never forget that. They all made me feel accepted and right at home from the start. Her brothers were all big sports fans, so that immediately gave us some good topics for conversations. Several of Cynthia's brothers had gone to Kansas State University. It would be an early test of our new relationship when I told them I had graduated from K.U., so I was relieved when they all started laughing about it. They all seemed like a pretty easygoing bunch. Overall, my initial encounter with Cynthia's family could not have gone much better.

There was definitely a lot to like about Cynthia and her family. The history of her family was simply amazing, as well. Their family's escape from the communists in Vietnam and their road to America is a story worthy of a book or a movie. It's a heroic story of a father's relentless pursuit of freedom and a better life for his family. To me, Cynthia's family represented the American dream. I know her family all really seemed to appreciate the freedoms and opportunities that America offered. They were all extremely hardworking and well educated. Several of Cynthia's five brothers had engineering degrees, and a couple of her sisters were college educated. Her oldest sister was also a very successful businesswoman. To their family, America offered

WITH GOD ALL THINGS ARE POSSIBLE!

possibilities that were endless and a future that had no boundaries.

I wasn't nearly as worried when it came time for Cynthia to meet my family. Cynthia always makes a good first impression because she has a great sense of humor. It doesn't hurt that she's attractive, either. On a Saturday afternoon, Cynthia and I went over to the house of my sister Rhonda and her husband, Oscar, for lunch. My mom and dad had come over to have lunch and to meet Cynthia as well. As I expected, everyone seemed to like Cynthia right from the start. My brother-in-law, Oscar, and Cynthia were joking with each other almost from the time we walked in the door. Oscar has a great sense of humor, too. He and I had been laughing together for nearly twenty years, ever since my sister and Oscar were first married. He's been a tremendous blessing to our family. My dad really liked Cynthia too. He and Cynthia shared a few laughs as well. So it looked like we were going to survive the sometimes very awkward first meetings with each other's families. I felt like both meetings were a huge success.

Every July 4th Cynthia, her kids, and I went to her brother Phillip's house to celebrate Independence Day. Most of Cynthia's nine brothers and sisters would usually come over, along with all of their children. Many times, we would go in their backyard and play baseball, volleyball, and other games. We would usually have steak or hamburgers cooked out on the grill, along with rice and some various kinds of healthy vegetables. Cynthia's family always ate very good and healthy food. They introduced me to all sorts of fruits and vegetables I had not even heard of. I liked most of them. Her family also tried to introduce me to chopsticks. You would think that if I could master Ping-Pong with only one hand, eating with chopsticks would be a breeze. I gave it my best, but my chopstick skills were not very good. I could chase one noodle around a bowl for three weeks with chopsticks and still never grab it. I had to eat with a fork. At around 9:00 p.m., we would all venture out to Phillip's front yard to watch the fireworks display put on in their neighborhood. It was always a memorable display and a great time. It wouldn't seem like anytime at all and we would be back the following year celebrating the fourth again.

Cynthia and I spent a lot of time together on the weekends taking two of her kids to their basketball and soccer games. Both Vivian, Cynthia's oldest daughter, and Vincent had either games or practices every weekend. I really enjoyed going to watch them play too. Seeing the joy on Cynthia's face when her kids scored a goal or made a basket was priceless. Cynthia loved her children more than anything in the whole world. It was beautiful and inspiring to see that. I wanted badly to be a part of that for a long time.

Cynthia's youngest daughter, Valine, would go along with us as well. She wasn't as interested in the sports activities early on. Cynthia would always call Valine her "little princess." Valine had inherited her mother's good looks and always said she wanted to grow up to be a model. She didn't take too well to me in the beginning. I could fully understand that, though, seeing that I was kind of taking their dad's place. I don't think I would have liked me much either. That got better as time went by.

After dating for three years it was time for me to ask Cynthia to get married. Obviously, she had been married before and knew all the challenges that marriage presented, but after three years of dating, I think we both felt like it was the right time to take the next step. So, I waited for a night when we were out to eat dinner by ourselves and somehow found the courage to ask her, "Cynthia, will you marry me?"

She didn't say yes. She said, "Okay," which was good enough for me. I was really excited, to say the least. I went home that night and called my parents and a few other choice friends and family members and told them my great news. I was getting married!

The next weekend, Cynthia and I were out shopping for those lovely and expensive little things called diamonds. We went everywhere from Kay Jewelers to Helzberg Diamonds, and I quickly received a crash course into a world that I had known very little about. I had never even heard of the four Cs of diamonds: cut, clarity, color, and carat. Cynthia, however, knew her diamonds like I knew my favorite sports teams. For me, buying a diamond ring was simply a necessary step for getting Cynthia to be my wife. For Cynthia, it was a whole different ball game. All I had to do was say the word "diamond" and I could see her face light up. Women like their diamonds.

Cynthia and I decided that we didn't want to spend a lot of money on a large wedding and all that goes with it. Cynthia had already experienced all of that with her first marriage, so she was just fine with having a very small wedding. That was fine with me too. I wanted Cynthia, not the big show. For me, the wedding wasn't a whole lot different than buying the diamond ring. It was just another step I had to go through to get to the prize, Cynthia as my wife. We could definitely use the money saved for other purposes too. We already had three kids to provide for and other needs as well. Spending a lot of money for one big day just didn't make a whole lot of sense to us.

On April 16, 2004, Cynthia and I were married at her home in Olathe, Kansas, in front of just a few special family and friends. It was a perfect day, and Cynthia couldn't have looked more beautiful. Our wedding could not have been any simpler. We simply had a judge come over to the house to perform the marriage ceremony. We both said our wedding vows, "For richer, for poorer, in sickness and in health, until death do us part." Then we all went out to eat and celebrated the new life and journey that Cynthia and I were about to begin. I could not have been any happier.

I really enjoyed my new life after getting married, but it immediately came with its share of challenges. Suddenly, I now had the responsibility of being a husband, a father, a coach, a referee, and whatever other job titles arose in the course of any given day. I was quickly immersed into a whole new world of self-denial that I had not experienced in my carefree, easygoing, it's-all-about-me single days. I learned really quickly that this marriage thing was going to force me to grow up in a big hurry, and that was a good thing. I needed to be forced to grow up and learn to live for and put others before myself. Marriage has a daily cross to bear. You either learn to deny yourself and live for your wife or you'll quickly be sleeping on the living room couch or, even worse, the kitchen floor. I'm only kidding, of course. Cynthia would never let me sleep on her shiny kitchen floor.

After saving our money for five years, Cynthia and I were ready to go out and purchase our dream home together. Ever since turning 30, I had dreamed of having a beautiful wife and a nice house to raise a family in. With interest rates at forty-year lows and after having finally saved enough money for the down payment, it was time to go out and make our dreams come true. Cynthia and I would quickly learn that buying a house can be one of the most stressful times that a married couple can go through together. We first contacted a real estate agent, and he immediately placed our current home on the market. We then went out on the internet and started the next-to-impossible task of trying to find the perfect house in the perfect neighborhood. I knew I wanted Cynthia to love the house that we ended up buying. My philosophy in marriage from the beginning was that if my wife was happy, then I was happy. Making my wife happy was always a good thing. Cynthia had really good taste, however, so I had full confidence that I would like whatever house she picked out.

Our old home was only be on the market for only two weeks before it sold for a price just under what we were asking. That was the good news. The bad news was that we would need to move out in just 30 days and we hadn't even found a home to buy yet. To say the least, our stress level went up a few notches. We were going to have to get real serious about our new-home search. We called our realtor and told him exactly what we were looking for and said we could take off of work if necessary to go out looking. Fortunately for us, within two weeks, he found us the home of our dreams. I could tell by Cynthia's reaction when she first walked into the house that it was the one. All of the kids would have their own bedrooms, a huge backyard to play in, and great schools to attend. We were home at last.

The kids really seemed to enjoy the new schools and quickly made quite a few friends around our neighborhood. Vincent was in junior high school. and the two girls were still in elementary school. One of my family duties was to help the kids with their homework when they needed it. I really enjoyed trying to remember and relearn all the things I had forgotten since I was in school. It brought back a lot of memories. In the evenings, I would help the kids with their homework while Cynthia was cooking dinner. Cynthia was an amazing cook. I honestly don't remember a meal that she made that I didn't like. After dinner, we would all usually have some time of rest and relaxation from a long day of work. Cynthia and I would take turns going up to the local YMCA to work out every other night. It was a great way for both of us to release some stress. Life was, all around, pretty sweet.

Our family life together had kind of a regular schedule to it. On Saturdays, we would usually go out to eat and either see a movie or go to a party at one of Cynthia's brother's or sister's houses. On Sundays we would go to Church and then head over to Cynthia's mom's house for lunch and to visit with her family. I would eventually begin to develop some pretty cool relationships with several members of her family. I really enjoyed the times that we would get together with Cynthia's family. How many people can honestly say that about their in-laws?

By August 2008, our life together could not have been better. We had been together for nearly eight years and married for more than four. We had the American Dream. We had good jobs, a beautiful house in a wonderful neighborhood with great schools, and three great-looking kids. We had everything the world says will provide eternal happiness and everlasting bliss. At that time, if you would have told me that within a year, my marriage would dissolve and I would be going through a divorce, I would have told you that you must have been talking about somebody else. But that is unfortunately what happened.

I have spent literally hundreds of hours ever since trying to break down where and how everything turned south so quickly. I still don't have all the answers. When a marriage fails, there are probably multiple reasons. We didn't have many fights. We had enough money. We didn't have any health issues. I guess if I could put my finger on one thing, it would be that over time, we may have let the romance die in our marriage. It's really easy when you're busy going to work, raising three teenage kids, doing chores, and just going through the daily stresses of life to forget to take time to love each other. For the last six months of the marriage, I could sense that the love may have slipped out of our marriage, but by that time, it was apparently too late. I may have taken my wife's love for granted. I knew that I would always love her, and I just assumed that she would always love me. When I tried to revive the romance during the last few months that we were together, my efforts were in vain. I was looking at the greatest failure in my life, and I remember crying out to God to help me. This was the one time in my life when God didn't seem to hear me.

The failure of my marriage and divorce was one of the most painful experiences I have ever had and probably will ever go through in my life. I would not wish it on anyone. I rolled the dice on love. I knew the risks going in and considered them worth it. I gave it everything I had, and I failed. But I didn't lose. With God, you can never lose. I will always love Cynthia. I'll always love her kids, too. I pray for them all the time. I pray for their success and happiness. I pray that they become doctors or lawyers or whatever God has destined them to be. I regret that my marriage with Cynthia ended. I regret that we didn't make it until death parted us. But I will never regret the relationship. I will never regret the nine years that we spent together. I'm a better man today because of it. I believe that God can take our failures in life and turn them around for our good and His glory. Romans 8:28 says, "And we know that in all things God works for the good of those who love

Him, who have been called according to His purpose." God is a redeemer. He can redeem us from any situation or tragedy in life as long as we trust in Him and never give up!

CHAPTER 6

Honor God, and He Will Honor You

I was raised in the Catholic Church. Every Sunday, my dad would take us down to St. Mark's Church in Independence, Missouri. It was there that I learned the foundational teachings of the Christian faith. One of the first doctrines that I learned was the truth that God is a trinity. The idea of the trinity is the doctrine that God is one and yet exists eternally in three persons: the Father, the Son, and the Holy Spirit. As I grew older, I learned that there are many practical evidences that the universe that we all live in was indeed created by a triune God. For example, the Bible says that God made man in His image so it would make sense that man would also be a trinity. We're made up of a body, a soul, and a spirit. Then it's interesting when you look at the makeup of time itself. It's made up of the past, present, and future. All colors in nature are made of only three primary colors: red, yellow, and blue. All the colors of the spectrum come from just those three. The analogy begins to break down a little here, but when you start studying the various elements in chemistry, you learn that many of them are made up of three parts. For instance, water, or H2O, is a chemical compound with one oxygen atom and two hydrogen atoms. Carbon dioxide, or CO2, is a chemical compound composed of two oxygen atoms and one carbon atom. The more you study the universe, the more it appears that the artist may have left His signature on His work.

One very interesting principle that I see at work in the triune God of the Bible is the desire for each person of the trinity to glorify the other. For instance, you see the Father's desire to glorify the Son. In John 8:54, Jesus replied, "If I glorify myself, my glory means nothing. My Father, whom you claim as your God, is the one who glorifies me." Then in other places, the Son seeks to bring glory to the Father. In John 12:27-28, for example, before being crucified, Jesus says, "Now my heart is troubled, and what shall I say? Father, save me from this hour? No, it was for this very reason I came to this hour. Father, glorify your name!" Then later the Holy Spirit seeks the glory of the Son. In John 16:26, Jesus, speaking about the Holy Spirit, said, "When the Counselor comes, whom I will send to you from the Father, the Spirit of Truth who goes out from the Father, he will testify about me." I believe that is how God wants all of our relationships in life to work, especially our relationship with Him, that we live our lives in such a way as to see that God is glorified and God in turn honors us in due time. That is one principle I try to live my life by. I certainly have plenty of character flaws and areas in my life where I need to

improve. God is still working on me and my character, but I believe God knows one thing about me: I
will confess Him before men even when it's unpopu-
lar, and I believe God has honored me for that. In
Romans 1:16, the Apostle Paul writes, "I am not
ashamed of the gospel, because it is the power of God
for the salvation of everyone who believes." Honor
God, and He will honor you.

In January 2010, Doug Hayden, a coworker of
mine at DST Systems, moved onto the same floor
and building I work at. He was a former diver at the
University of Nebraska and had set many swimming
records in the Kansas City Corporate Challenge.
The Kansas City Corporate Challenge is an annual
corporate Olympic event with companies competing
from all over the Kansas City area in just about every
sport imaginable. The event began back in 1980 with
only 15 companies and has grown today to include
more than 150 companies. I had met Doug at the
KCCC Awards Banquet a couple of years earlier in
2008 when I had been nominated for the Alex George
Award. I knew he was a great athlete, and, to be honest, I expected him to be a little full of himself. He
turned out to be one of the nicest, funniest, most
down-to-earth guys I've ever met.

Doug came to my desk in January and asked me,
"Why don't we try to win the Corporate Challenge as
a company and resubmit your nomination for the
Alex George Award?" I told him that it sounded like
a great idea and we should start making plans immediately. I told him that I needed to broaden my
resume, however, if I was going to be qualified to win

the Alex George Award. I knew from past winners of the award that the KCCC board of directors generally liked people to be broadly involved by participating in many sports. So I told Doug to think of some other sports, other than table tennis, that a triple amputee could be good at.

There's one thing you have to understand about Doug. Other than his beautiful wife and his two great-looking kids, Doug's mind is concerned really with only one thing: swimming. Outside of his full-time job at DST Systems, Doug coaches a masters swim team and gives swimming lessons at the Gladstone Community Center. The center is about ten minutes from where he lives in North Kansas City.

Doug came to my desk a few hours later and asked, "Could you swim the fifty-yard freestyle?"

I immediately laughed to myself and then replied, "Doug, mothers take their children to these swim meets. I have only one arm and no legs. I have no legs, Doug. Do you want them to have to put ratings on all the Corporate Challenge sporting events next year?" We both laughed out loud. Then I hesitated for a second, and for a reason only God knew at the time, I responded, "But I did used to swim laps back in college." Doug jumped all over those words, and a few weeks later, we began meeting at the pool to train for a swim that neither one of us will likely ever forget, not in this lifetime anyway.

DST Systems competes in Division A, with companies with 2500 or more employees. Some of our big competitors include Sprint, Garmin, Cerner, Hallmark Cards, and Black & Veatch. We knew we had our work cut out for us if we were going to come in first. In the past couple of years, however, DST had finished only 50 and 80 points out of first, with the winner having around 800 points total. It was a gap that we believed we could close if we worked hard enough and implemented the right strategies.

I had competed in the Kansas City Corporate Challenge since 1992. The three sporting events I had competed in were the basketball shootout, the football throw, and, of course, table tennis. In 2010, I would add swimming to the list. I honestly would have competed in several more events over the years, but it's not at all easy to make the team. When you compete in a company with several thousand employees, just qualifying for your corporate team can be quite an accomplishment. I remember the year I was able to represent my company in the football throw. I had gone to the event with all the confidence in the world. I felt like I had a pretty good arm and was ready to show everybody what I had. I had gone out there and started warming up, trying to throw the ball at a target that was thirty yards away. I was able to hit it a couple of times with a bit of an arc on the ball. At that time, I was feeling really good about myself. My confidence would not last long, however. A few moments later, this guy came up beside me and grabbed a ball and threw it thirty yards on a line and hit the target right in the center. I immediately walked over and asked the guy, "Are you John Elway?" He laughed. Then he told me he had played quarterback in college at a Division II school. Wow! That was an eye-opening experience for me. Trust me, those guys we see playing football on television on the weekends make it look easy. As it turned out, I didn't do that great in the football-throw event. I believe I was tenth out of 16 participants.

Another year, I qualified to represent my company in the basketball shootout. This event was quite the challenge. We had two one-minute rounds to score as many points as we could from various spots on the court. The part that was especially difficult for me was running down the rebounds when I missed so it was extremely critical for me to shoot the ball well. The ball doesn't run very far away from you when it goes through the bottom of the net. Just like in the football throw, I witnessed a guy competing in the event who would bring me back to reality about my apparent basketball skills. This guy was amazing. He had this event down to a sports science. There was one place on the court that he took almost all of his shots from. It was a 16-foot shot that counted for four points. This guy made every shot from that spot, and before the ball could even hit the ground, he had caught it and was racing back to the same spot again to shoot. I honestly think Michael Jordan would have had his hands full beating this guy in that particular event. I know he was clearly out of my league. He ended up winning the gold with a score of 99 points for his two rounds. I came in 11th out of 16 participants with a score of 52. I got schooled.

My best sport over the years in the Kansas City Corporate Challenge has been, far and away, table tennis. Going into 2010, my overall record was 52-7 playing either singles or doubles. I had won six singles titles and three doubles titles. My greatest victory had come over the ninth-ranked player in the state of Kansas. I describe that match in detail in Chapter 7, "Do You Believe in Miracles?" My greatest loss came against the highest-rated player in the state of Missouri. Playing doubles always presented a much bigger challenge for me than singles. In doubles table tennis, you have to alternate hits with your partner while moving in and out from the table. Playing with prosthetic legs can result in some interesting points, especially once my opponents figure out that I don't have any legs.

The four years preceding 2010, I played doubles with my friend and DST coworker Anand Mehta. Over those four years, we compiled a record in Division A of 13-2, winning two gold and two silver medals. Anand and I make an excellent doubles team because our strengths complement each other perfectly. Anand has some of the best serves in the Kansas City area. He has serves that can make grown men cry. His serves have much spin on them, and he mixes them up very effectively. He also possesses an excellent forehand smash shot. I have some excellent short serves as well, but the strength of my game is defense and ball placement. Being able to place the ball precisely where you want to on the table really comes in handy in the doubles table tennis game.

One of our most memorable doubles matches was in the 2005 semifinals against one of our biggest rivals, Sprint. Anand and I had just beaten Cerner easily, three games to none in the match prior, so we came in with a lot of momentum and confidence.

Sprint had an excellent doubles team that had a history of doing very well in table tennis. Anand and I started out playing great and won the first two games fairly easily. If you had asked me at that moment how many games that match would go, I would have probably told you three. I would have been wrong. Sprint started playing a lot better and started hitting the ball away from me so I would have a difficult time getting to it. Sprint won the next two games to even up the best-of-five-game match 2-2. In the decisive game, Sprint continued their momentum and took a commanding 9-3 advantage. It did not look good for us guys from DST. In all my years of playing, I don't remember another situation that ever looked so dark. Anand and I laugh about it now, but at that time, we both thought we were dead. Call it luck, fate, destiny, or a miracle: whatever it was, we will never forget it. Anand and I scored nine out of the last ten points to win, 12-10. We then advanced to the final, where we would beat KCP&L for the gold medal.

To be fair, the same Sprint doubles team got their revenge the next year when we met in the final. It was in the first game that Anand and I blew the match. We had a 7-4 lead and were playing excellently. Somehow, we must have lost our concentration for a moment, because we ended up losing game one 11-9. We split the next two games, giving Sprint the lead two games to one. Game four turned out to be quite a battle. I remember it as being one of most competitive games I was ever a part of in the Kansas City Corporate Challenge. I think a big reason for that was that I hated to lose and I knew we were in deep trouble. We won game four, 11-8. The match was back to two games each. The fifth game would decide the gold medal. I don't know what happened to us in game five. Sprint scored the first seven points. It would have been a little too much to expect to pull off a miracle comeback two years in a row. It didn't happen. Congratulations to Sprint.

Doug and I met together in February 2010 with several other committed Corporate Challenge athletes to begin to put together our strategy for victory. Our strategy was simple: recruit new athletes to fill holes left unfilled in previous years then get those athletes excited about winning the Corporate Challenge together as a company. This was going to be the year that Sprint and Cerner had to accept something other than first- and second-place finishes. We had quite a few new young employees in our building at work who looked pretty athletic. I was determined to not let those nice, young, healthy bodies go to waste. I told all of them that they looked like amazing athletes. Most of them did, of course. I told people that the Corporate Challenge was a wonderful way to meet new friends and have fun even if they weren't great athletes. I have honestly met some of my best friends by competing in the Corporate Challenge. Within a week of starting, I had recruited quite a few athletes to fill previously unfilled slots on our DST company team. Doug was having a lot of success recruiting people as well. I felt like we were getting people excited and optimistic too. We needed to get people believing that this was going to be our big breakthrough year at DST. We were not going to be denied.

Besides recruiting for the Corporate Challenge, Doug and I had to train hard to prepare to win our own personal sporting events. Doug was the best swimmer on the DST swim team. He owned four Corporate Challenge records out of a possible six in the 40-44 year-old-age group. He had the 50-yard freestyle record, the 50- yard butterfly record, the 100-yard individual medley record, and the 200-yard freestyle record. The only two events that he did not have the record for were the 50-yard breaststroke and the 50-yard backstroke. This year, Doug would be looking to set all new records in the 45-49 year-old-age group, having recently turned 45. Training to win that many types of swimming events requires a lot of hard work and talent. We knew that if we were going to do well in the swim meet and in the Corporate Challenge overall, Doug had to carry us. Doug believed that setting four records was an obtainable goal for him, with an outside shot at five. The 50-yard breaststroke was the only event that he conceded that he had no realistic shot at winning or setting a record in.

I would be competing in the 50-yard freestyle swimming event and the doubles table tennis event with my partner, Anand Mehta. Winning the gold medal is always our goal, but we knew we would have plenty of competition this year. The doubles table tennis competition in Division A in 2010 would come down to DST, Sprint, Garmin, and Cerner. Whoever played their best would probably win. Anand and I started practicing around the middle of February. We had a good strategy. We both worked hard to get our bodies in great shape. I was starting to swim around that time, so it would provide great cross-training for my table tennis game, and Anand ran several miles each day. The other piece of our strategy was to work hard on our serves and service returns. We figured if we got all of our opponents' serves back and then earned a few easy points off our own serves, we would have an excellent chance for success.

Anand and I won our first two doubles matches in 2010 relatively easily. We won both our first two matches three games to zero. That set us up for a showdown with Cerner in the semifinals. The other semifinal match had Sprint going up against Garmin. Cerner always did well in most sports in the Corporate Challenge, and table tennis was no exception. The 2009 and 2010 table tennis singles champion was from Cerner, and Cerner's doubles team was solid too. Anand and I felt as prepared for this year's competition as we had ever been. We were both in great shape physically and had a solid game plan going in. We just had to execute. Cerner started out playing extremely well, though, and before Anand and I knew what hit us, we had lost game one 11-8. Losing the first game in a best-three-of-five-game match is often fatal. We both knew that we had to win game two if we were going to advance and have a shot at the gold medal. Cerner did not let up, though. They played very solid table tennis and made us earn every single point. In the second game, we managed to finally get ahead of them 10-8 on the back of Anand's great serves. On the next point, it appeared that we were going to win the game when Cerner popped a ball straight up high in the air. Anand's overhand smash clipped the top of the net, however, and went just off the end of the table. The score was now 10-9 and my heart was beating very nervously. Fortunately for us, Cerner's next service return went long, giving us a critical 11-9 win in game two. The match was now tied one to one. At this point, it felt like Anand and I had just dodged a huge bullet, and I think we both breathed a big sigh of relief that we were not down 2-0. We went on to win games three and four easily and to advance to the finals against our rival, Sprint. We would be facing the same Sprint team that had beaten us in five games the last time we had met in the finals. This time, however, Anand and I would be ready for them.

Game one against Sprint was the critical game in my mind. In our prior matches with Sprint, the winner of game one had gone on to win the match. We won the right to serve first, and just like in every other match, I gave the ball to Anand to get us started. My serves are pretty good, but they're not nearly as deceptive as Anand's. His serves can win matches. True to form, Anand got us off to a flying start by getting the first two points of the match. For one reason or another, Sprint never really settled into their game, and we won game one 11-5. Anand and I went on to play probably our best match ever, easily winning games two and three and winning the gold medal. That added another 12 points to DST's point total. I had one tough sporting event behind me, with one to go. Next, it would be off to the swim meet and my long-awaited date with destiny.

The Kansas City Corporate Challenge Swim Meet was held from June 21 through June 24. Doug would be competing on all four days in eight swimming events. I would just be swimming in the 50-yard freestyle event. Mentally, though, I might as well have been swimming 20 events. I was nervous going into my first competitive swim, and cheering for Doug would help calm me. My swim is described later in detail in Chapter 7, "Do You Believe in Miracles?"

As I said before, Doug had his eyes set on setting four records and had an outside shot at getting five. Monday would be Doug's first shot at a gold medal and a new Corporate Challenge record when he would compete in the 200-yard freestyle swimming event. This event is long enough that setting the right pace can be a critical factor. If a swimmer starts out too fast, he might just not have enough left in the tank to finish strong. Doug was a seasoned veteran, however: I got the impression that he could swim some of these races in his sleep and probably did. He kicked off our 2010 DST Swim Meet with a new Corporate Challenge record in the 200-yard freestyle event. His time was 1:55.30, beating the old record of 1:56.73 in the 45-49 age group. That was an exciting way to get it started.

On Tuesday, Doug competed in the 50-yard breaststroke and the 100-yard individual medley events. He had hoped both to win a gold medal and to set another Corporate Challenge record in the 100-yard individual medley. He did end up winning another gold medal but came up just 14 one hundredths of a second short of a new record with a time of 59.64 seconds. There is not a lot of margin for error in the sport of swimming, especially when competing near the top. I know that race was a bit of a disappointment for Doug, but at least it left him with some unfinished business to motivate him for the next year.

Doug had only one event on Wednesday, the 50-yard freestyle event or 50 yards of madness, as Doug and I like to call it. It basically amounts to a wild scramble: eight guys lining up to see who wants it most. Once again, Doug apparently wanted it most: he won another gold medal and set another new Corporate Challenge record with a time of 23.35 seconds. The old record was 23.60 seconds.

On Thursday, Doug finished by swimming the 50-yard butterfly and the 50-yard backstroke events. He wasn't too happy with his performance in the 50-yard backstroke, as he came in with a time of 28.69 seconds. That was about a second slower than he had been hoping for. The 50-yard butterfly event turned out much better. Doug swam another amazing race and set his third Corporate Challenge record with a time of 25.55.

Despite Doug's usual great performances, DST did not have its best year in the swim meet. The final swim meet results were Cerner first, Children's Mercy Hospitals and Clinics second, Hallmark Cards third, Sprint fourth, and DST fifth. We also did not end up achieving our corporate goal of coming in first in Division A for the Kansas City Corporate Challenge. The final results were Cerner first, Sprint second, DST third, Hallmark Cards fourth, and Garmin fifth. DST finished just 78 points out of first place. We did, however, have a great time trying. Doug and I always make sure that we have a good time and plenty of laughs along the way. I made sure that I met lots of great people and made several new friends as well. That is the best part about the Corporate Challenge. Not reaching all of our goals simply means we're going to have to work harder next year. Doug and I will probably have to start recruiting people in January instead of February. I can't wait.

The following Tuesday, Doug was back at work, putting the finishing touches on my Alex George Award for Excellence write-up that he would submit to the KCCC Board of Directors. We had come up a little short in our goal of winning the Corporate Challenge as a company, but we were hoping that we might be able to still win the Alex George Award. The Alex George Award is presented each year to two athletes, one male and one female. The qualifications considered for the award are athletic ability, ability to overcome obstacles performing athletic events, dedication to the KCCC in organizing and promoting events, selflessness in dealings with KCCC, and sportsmanship. Doug had the difficult task of trying to convince the KCCC Board of Directors that a guy like me was qualified for anything, let alone the most prestigious award one could win in the Corporate Challenge. I was praying for Doug around the clock. All kidding aside, though, I really wanted to win the award. I had reminded Doug that there was no Corporate Challenge record book for sports like table tennis and that if my achievements were ever going to be recorded, I would need to win the Alex George Award so for me, winning the award would kind of be like getting inducted into the Corporate Challenge Hall of Fame. What athlete wouldn't want that?

When I came back from lunch that Tuesday, June 29, Doug about scared me to death when he pointed to the Alex George Award nomination form in the KCCC magazine. It stated that the deadline for submitting a nomination was Monday, June 28. I could not believe my eyes. My heart skipped a couple of beats. "You have got to be kidding me," I said in disbelief. I could see it now. We had just spent six months working harder than we had probably worked in our entire lives, and now we would be disqualified because we had printed off the wrong form. Evidently, the KCCC website had not been updated yet and the form Doug and I had been using still said the deadline was June 29, 2009. It should have read June 28, 2010. So Doug quickly sent an email to Katie Roder, the Executive Director for the Kansas City Corporate Challenge, explaining and pleading our pathetic case. It must have been the longest 30-minute wait for a response that I can ever remember. Katie emailed Doug back, apologizing for the form on the website not being updated and then stating that they would accept my nomination form a day late. My heart started beating again. The impossible dream was still alive!

Katie Roder emailed Doug the very next day and told him that this year had one of the most impressive group of nominees for the Alex George Award that she could ever remember. She then went on to say that the KCCC Board of Directors had chosen me to be the male 2010 Alex George Award winner and would honor me two weeks later at the KCCC Awards Banquet. Doug later told me that he had been so excited by the news that he had almost fallen out of his chair at work. The major problem that Doug was then faced with was trying to keep that incredibly exciting news away from me. Doug and I had just spent the past six months sharing absolutely everything with one another. I knew everything about Doug, from what he ate for breakfast each day to what time he finally went to bed at night. The odds of Doug being able to keep a secret of that magnitude from me were not very good.

The next couple of weeks were an emotional roller coaster for me. I went from one emotional extreme to the next. One day I would begin to feel confident that we were going to win. The next day, I would fear that we hadn't done enough to deserve the award. I probably drove Doug nuts over the two-week period, coming to his desk and asking him whether he thought we had won. Doug just kept his poker face on, trying not to give me any hint of what he already knew. Finally, I remember turning it all over to God and saying, "Thy will be done." It was only then that I had peace in my heart.

The KCCC Awards Banquet would be held on Friday, July 16 at the Hyatt Regency Crown Center Hotel in Kansas City, Missouri. In only its 31st year, the Kansas City Corporate Challenge had become an incredible success story and a sporting event envied all around the country. I believe much of the key to its success has been due to the high-quality, selfless people who run the organization. I know that the Kansas City Corporate Challenge has been a tremendous blessing to not only me, but also the entire Kansas City metro area community.

Doug, my brother-in-law, Oscar, and I drove over together to the KCCC awards banquet. We arrived around 5:30 p.m. At this point, I still had no idea that Doug knew I had won the award. He had done an incredible job of keeping me in the dark. I honestly believed that we had a decent chance of winning, but I was not going to set myself up to be disappointed. I had told Oscar and Doug on the way over to the banquet that I was going to have a great time no matter what the results ended up being. As far as I was concerned, it was all in God's hands.

Around 6:00 p.m., we all headed upstairs to get seated for the dinner and the presentation of the awards. Approximately six hundred people were attending the event. Katie Roder, the Executive Director of the KCCC kicked off the 2010 KCCC Awards Banquet with the announcement, "Dave is in the house." She was talking, of course, about Dave Stewart, the very funny and popular local sports broadcaster of Metro Sports, a regional sports network. Dave Stewart had always been one of my favorite sports broadcasters, bringing me all the latest news on my favorite local sports teams: the Kansas City Royals, the Kansas City Chiefs, and the Kansas Jayhawks. The thought of a guy like Dave Stewart reading my write-up if I were to win the Alex George Award was a bit overwhelming. I can't think of anyone around the country I would rather have to present something about me than Dave Stewart. He is extremely talented and gifted. I have to admit, though, it's a little difficult saying nice things about a guy who graduated from Kansas State University, K.U.'s arch rival. Even though Jesus did command us to love our enemies, there are times in life when that can be a bit of a challenge. Not in this case, however. Dave Stewart is one of the coolest guys you'll ever meet.

After we had all finished with dinner, Dave Stewart came back on stage to begin the award presentation portion of the KCCC Awards Banquet. He went through all the divisions and presented awards for places first through eighth. DST came in third in Division A, and our teammate and coworker Denise Davis went up to graciously receive our trophy. We were all happy but not satisfied. We will definitely give it another shot next year.

Next, it was finally the moment of truth. It was time to announce the two winners of the 2010 KCCC Alex George Award. Dave Stewart started off with the female category. He first listed all of the female nominees, who all came up one at a time to get their awards. Then Mr. Stewart read the write-up about the winner. The female winner of the 2010 Alex George Award was Julie Lawrence from CSS/IAAP/PIVOT. Congratulations, Julie! Next, Dave Stewart started calling, one by one the names of all the male nominees, and we went up and got our awards. By this time, I was really nervous. In just a couple of moments, I would find out if my dreams of making it into the Corporate Challenge Hall of Fame were going to come true. I looked over at Doug, who still had his poker face on. Dave Stewart then started reading the winning write-up: "Our male nominee was born with only one arm, and no legs below the knees." The manner in which Dave Stewart presented my write-up had many people in the crowd crying. By the ninth word, I obviously knew I had won. At that time I remember a lot of different emotions coming over me at the same time. I wanted to thank everyone: God, my parents, Doug, the KCCC Board of Directors, and all the people who had helped me through the years to get to this day. It was a moment I will never forget. It was at this time that my parents came up from behind me to give me a big hug. I had not expected my parents to be there because the banquet is reserved for corporate participants. That was a huge surprise that Doug had arranged in the week prior to the banquet. Having my parents there made the moment all the more special.

The entire write-up that Doug submitted for my nomination for the Alex George Award read as follows:

> *"Tim Clark was born with only one arm, and no legs below the knees. His parents' greatest dreams were for Tim to walk, and live a "normal" life. He likes to take on challenges as an example of what anyone can do if they believe. He doesn't*

do it to appear normal, rather, because he IS normal. He once even ran a 10K au naturale, on his knees, in less than 1.5 hours!

Table tennis is Tim's sport of choice. Imagine trying to play table tennis wearing stilts. Now, tie one arm behind your back! How will you serve? These are the challenges Tim faces every time he plays.

Tim has been a dominating force in KCCC table tennis since 1992. Every year he participates, he brings honor to the games. His overall KCCC record is 56-7, winning 10 gold and 5 silver medals in either singles or doubles. 2010 was no exception. He and his partner once again won gold in Division A doubles. Tim is also an avid recruiter for all KCCC events, volunteer, and table tennis coach.

He also participates in other KCCC events. This year, Tim took on one of his biggest challenges as a first time swimmer! He attacked his training with fierce dedication. He said, "I don't want to be the disabled guy that did ok. I want to compete!"

When Tim stepped out of his comfort zone, and onto the pool deck, he was admittedly "scared to death!" Cheering for fellow DST swimmers calmed his nerves. Tim set aside his inhibitions and his prosthetic legs, quietly slipped into lane one, and swam 50 free in just 45.25 seconds. Everyone lucky enough to witness Tim's race was awe struck!

Tim is a mild mannered, humble hero who is quick to give the glory to God. He doesn't like to hear that he is "AMAZING," but that is the word so many of his teammates, competitors, and total strangers use to describe him. He is just the normal guy born with only one arm, no legs, and a heart of gold that inspires us all.

Besides playing sports, one of the many things I like to do is keep up on all the latest news that affects our nation and our world. We are definitely living in challenging and uncertain times that test the souls of people all around the world. As a Christian, I try to look at myself first and then at the Church to see where we can improve and provide solutions to the problems that we all face. One of my favorite pastors and authors in America is Rick Warren. He was the moderator for the 2008 presidential debate between

Barack Obama and John McCain. He wrote the best-selling book *The Purpose Driven Life*, one of the best books I have ever read. I have heard Rick Warren predict that a revival in the church in America is coming. I hope he is right. I believe that we need one. I believe we need to stop looking to Washington for the right Democrat or Republican to fix all of the many problems we face in America. I believe we need to look no further than to awaken that sleeping giant known as the Church of Jesus Christ.

Jesus told believers (the Church) that we are the salt and light of the world. In Matthew 5:13, Jesus says, "You are the salt of the earth. But if the salt loses its saltiness, how can it be made salty again? It is no longer good for anything, except to be thrown out and trampled by men." Then Jesus continues in Matthew 5:14-16 "You are the light of the world. A city on a hill cannot be hidden. Neither do people light a lamp and put it under a bowl. Instead they put it on its stand, and it gives light to everyone in the house. In the same way, let your light shine before men, that they may see your good deeds and praise your father in heaven." Jesus indicated that when the church is no longer salt and light, it becomes good for nothing. One of the big responsibilities that God has given the church is to be both a moral- preserving force to society and a light to people showing them the right path to follow. Unfortunately, when the church fails to live up to her calling, society begins the inevitable slide toward moral relativism and confusion. As someone has so eloquently put it, when the church catches a cold, society gets pneumonia.

elieve we need a revival in the church in Amer-
ilar to the one that occurred in what historians
call the First Great Awakening. That was a spiritual
revival that occurred in the American Colonies in the
1730s and 1740s. This revival in the church in America was part of a bigger movement among evangelicals
going on in England, Scotland, and Germany. The
common theme amidst this movement in Protestant
churches was a new Age of Faith to go against its con-
temporary Age of Enlightenment. The idea that arose
was that it was wiser to trust the heart than the head
and to trust in biblical revelation instead of human rea-
soning. One of the main clergymen leading this movement was a preacher by the name of Jonathan
Edwards. In his famous sermon, "Sinners in the
Hands of an Angry God" Edwards described in great
detail the corruption in human nature and the future of
all sinners who chose not to repent. Another influen-
tial figure in the First Great Awakening was an English
preacher by the name of George Whitefield. Whitefield preached all over the American Colonies. He
preached what many Calvinists had proclaimed for
centuries, that men were totally dependent on a merci-
ful, all-powerful God to save them.

If it is indeed the Church that has led us into the
mess that America appears to be in, I believe the
Church can lead us out. In 2 Chronicles 7:14, God
promises, "If my people, who are called by my name,
will humble themselves and pray and seek my face
and turn from their wicked ways, then will I hear
from heaven and will forgive their sin and will heal
their land."

When I look at the many problems America faces today, including a national debt approaching 15 trillion dollars, I fear we may have put ourselves under the curse Moses spoke about in the Book of Deuteronomy. One can't help but see a lot of parallels between ancient Israel and the modern United States of America. In Deuteronomy 28, Moses lays out to the nation of Israel all the blessings that will follow them if they obey God. Then he lists all the curses that will come to them if they don't. It's a little scary. It sounds a lot like the nightly news I turn on before I go to bed every night. Deuteronomy 28:43-44 says, "The alien who lives among you will rise above you higher, but you will sink lower and lower. He will lend to you, but you will not lend to him. Sounds a lot like budget deficits. He will be the head, but you will be the tail." It gets worse in verses 47-50. "Because you did not serve the Lord your God joyfully and gladly in the time of prosperity, therefore in hunger and thirst, in nakedness and dire poverty, you will serve the enemies the Lord sends against you. He will put an iron yoke on your neck until he has destroyed you. The Lord will bring a nation against you from far away, from the ends of the earth, like an eagle swooping down, a nation whose language you will not understand, a fierce-looking nation without respect for the old or pity for the young."

I love this country and would not have wanted to be born anywhere else, but I believe we may have chosen to go down a wrong road somewhere along the way. The principle of honoring God so He will honor you applies to nations as well as to individuals. Unfortunately, history is filled with examples of nations who have left God and paid the ultimate price. When a nation begins to turn away from God, freedoms begin to evaporate. The good news is, I don't believe God ever left America. I believe we have left Him. I believe He is waiting with open arms to take us back. The choice is ours. I hope and pray that America's best days are ahead of her. I hope we return again to being that great City on a Hill that the pilgrim John Winthrop spoke about. I pray that when we look back at history, we see this period as a time when America faced a crossroad and chose the road of faith in God and freedom. Wake up, America. *With God, All Things Are Possible!*

CHAPTER 7

Do You Believe in Miracles?

I t was a beautiful Sunday morning on April 24, 1988. In only its second year, the Dillards/Nike 10k had 1500 runners in Kansas City, Missouri. I had trained for six months to prepare for the biggest athletic challenge of my young life. Little did I know at the time that this event when I was 20 would end up being my life's greatest athletic achievement (hence, the picture on the cover of the book). I was trying to run a 10k on my knees, without prosthetics, in less than 1.5 hours. I don't believe anyone had ever done anything like that before or has since. To be honest, I don't believe anyone has been dumb enough to try. Just to give you an idea of what I was attempting to pull off, try running across your family room floor on your knees. Then imagine trying to go 6.2 miles in less than 1.5 hours on pavement. I had only a specially made pad to cover my right knee and a shoe turned around backward to fit over my left knee. I was used to running on my knees. I had run around on my knees all my life-just never for any real distance. The race just happened to be exactly 20 days after I had cheered "Danny and the Miracles" on to the national title. Having that in the back of my mind helped with the mental game. My training consisted of swimming, running, and wrestling. This was around the time I was in the K.U. Wrestling Club. Swimming played a big part in getting me in condition for this race. I never swam for speed but for distance, and that really conditioned my heart and lungs. I worked up to swimming a mile in the pool nearly every day prior to my 10k race. I was running only about two miles per day. In fact, prior to the race, the most I had ever run was 5k, or 3.1 miles.

The weather for the 10k could not have been nicer. We had no wet, slick roads or anything like that to contend with. I simply had to focus on the task at hand and cross the finish line a short 6.2 miles away. This was my second road race ever. I had run a 5k in Lawrence, Kansas, some eight months earlier, but this was the bigger by far, with 1500 participants signed up.

The gun sounded, and we were off. I was obviously near the back so as to not get run over by the big crowd. I usually ran a mile on my knees in about 14 minutes, so that was the pace I wanted to set. I reached the one-mile mark at 14:12, so I was just about right on schedule. My body felt good, and my mind was focused on the long road ahead. One of the good things about this particular course was that it had a lot of downhill the last two miles. I knew if I could just get to the last couple miles in decent shape, I would have a chance.

The people running this race and the police did an unbelievable job in dealing with my unique running situation. I had a police car escort driving right alongside me through the entire race to make sure I didn't get hit by any traffic or need any medical attention. I certainly hadn't expected it, but it was certainly nice, and what the police would later do for me near the end of the race was simply off the charts. (I don't want to spoil the ending by telling you yet, though.)

I completed the second mile at the 28:50 mark-a little slower than I would have liked, but my body still felt pretty good. There weren't any other runners around me, just the police escort and people standing on the side of the road, cheering me on, and race volunteers handing me water to drink. I drank lots of water. I did not want to take any chance on dehydration. As I approached the three-mile mark, I had a sense of optimism that my dream of running a 10k in under 1.5 hours on my knees was going to happen.

I crossed the three-mile mark at 43:32. I was nearly halfway home, with much of the last two miles being downhill. As I ran, I was amazed at the number of people still standing and cheering for me on the side of the road. Someone must have passed word that a disabled runner was running the race on his knees.

As I approached the fourth mile, I felt my body starting to get tired. I was slowing down a bit. I crossed the four-mile mark at 58:01. I was right on track-2.2 miles left and about thirty minutes to get there. This was farther than I had ever run before, though. I was in uncharted waters, and my body felt like it. The police officer driving right alongside me kept giving me words of encouragement. I remember him saying that I only had a couple miles left and this was going to be special.

The pain was really kicking in by the time I reached the five-mile mark at 1:12:25. Despite all the water I had drunk, I believe I started to get a little dehydrated. I remember feeling lightheaded and my body screaming at me to stop. There was no way I was going to quit, though. I had run more than five miles on my knees, and mentally, I could see the finish line. When I reached the 5.5-mile point, the police officer told me that they were setting up a police motorcade in front of me for the last quarter of a mile. I thought, *Wow! This is going to be cool!*

When I got around a quarter of a mile from the finish line, about eight police motorcycles pulled out in front of me. I couldn't believe it! It was so awesome that they were nice enough to do that. Obviously, at that point, the adrenaline kicked in. I could hear the crowd cheering for me at the finish line. I had a police motorcade in front of me. I kind of felt like the president of the United States for a moment; here I was, just a disabled guy running a 10k on my knees. I couldn't believe they had done all that for me. At that point, I was running fast. For the last hundred yards, I probably ran as fast as I'd ever run. I crossed the finish line in 1 hour, 28 minutes, and 14 seconds! To this day, I can still hear the crowd cheering as I finished. What a moment! What a feeling! Do I believe in miracles? Yes!

Jerry Smith, a reporter for the running magazine *Masterpiece* described my race: "By far the most impressive performance in this race and in any race I've witnessed in a long time was turned in by a young disabled runner. He was a young man, probably in his early twenties, with both legs amputated about halfway between the knee and hip and with only one good arm. This determined individual ran the entire way and finished in less than 1 ½ hours. It was a sight to behold as he was running without the aid of any artificial limbs or any other type of device. Seeing this athlete coming down the road with his eyes and mind seemingly completely focused on running the race and giving it his all was enough to bring chills to anyone. This courageous young man is to be congratulated on a fantastic race."

I've been a fan of all kinds of sports my whole life, but no story still inspires me today like the 1980 U.S. Olympic hockey team's victory over the Soviets and their subsequent gold medal. In the middle of the cold war, with the economy in turmoil and gas prices through the roof, a bunch of college kids inspired a nation like nothing I've seen since. There are many lessons to be learned from that incredible success story. Underdogs from that day on have taken heart that they too can pull off the impossible and be great for at least a moment in time. Herb Brooks, the coach of the U.S. hockey team in 1980, was a master motivator and a genius at getting his players to believe in themselves and one another. He too had been an underdog and had to persevere through adversity in his life. In 1960, the last year the U.S. had won the Olympic gold in hockey, Herb Brooks had been the last player cut from the team. That year, after the U.S. had completed its gold-medal run, Herb's father suggested to Herb that they must have cut the right guy. One can only guess that those comments lit a fire under Herb Brooks and motivated him to become one of the greatest coaches of all time.

To start the 1980 games, the U.S. faced heavily favored Sweden. Going into the games, the U.S. had been picked around fifth by many seeding the tournament. Late in the third period, the U.S. trailed Sweden 2-1. With less than 45 seconds left in the game, Herb Brooks pulled Jim Craig from the goal. The desperate move paid off, as the extra offensive player, Billy Baker, slapped in a game-tying shot with just 28 seconds left. A 2-2 tie instead of a loss kept the U.S. dreams alive.

Two days later, the U.S. faced Czechoslovakia in a second-round game. Once again, the U.S. would be the underdogs in a game that they had to win. To the surprise of many, the U.S. beat Czechoslovakia 7-3. The U.S. then won three games that they were favored in. They beat Norway and Romania fairly easily. West Germany put up more of a fight, leading the Americans 2-0 before the U.S. came storming back to win. Then it was on to the medal round to face the Soviet Union. The long-awaited dream match was about to happen.

What a sports story! No one in the world gave the Americans a chance. Not long before the Olympics, the Soviets had beaten an NHL All-Star team 6-0. It was not a matter of if the Soviets would win the gold medal but by how much. But the Americans had a

WITH GOD ALL THINGS ARE POSSIBLE!

coach who believed in the impossible. They had a coach who dared to believe in what others said could not happen, and little by little, Herb Brooks got his players to believe it too. Herb began saying to his players, "Somebody's going to beat these guys. They're too cocky. Somebody's going to beat these guys." In one of the most inspiring pregame speeches in sports history, Herb Brooks planted the seeds of the 1980 Lake Placid miracle in the hearts of his young hockey warriors: "Great moments are born from great opportunities. That's what you have here tonight, boys. That's what you've earned here tonight. One game. If we played them ten times they might win nine, but not this game. Not tonight. Tonight we skate with them. Tonight we stay with them, and we shut them down because we can. Tonight we are the greatest hockey team in the world. You were born to be hockey players, every one of you. And you were meant to be here tonight. This is your time. Their time is done. It's over. I'm sick and tired of hearing about what a great hockey team the Soviets have. Screw em! This is your time! Now go out there and take it!"

The Americans came out playing inspired hockey against the Soviets. They came out with an energy they had not shown in the exhibition game a few weeks earlier. Even still, the Soviets scored the first goal around the 9:10 mark of the first period. Jim Craig then made some very big saves, and a few minutes later, the U.S. scored a goal to tie the score at 1-1. Not long after that, the Soviets scored again to make it 2-1, but then the Soviets made a mental mistake late in the first period.

With around five seconds to go, the Soviet players just kind of stopped playing. The puck got sent down into the Soviet end, where Mark Johnson of the U.S. grabbed it and scored with one second left in the period so instead of the first period ending with the U.S. down 2-1, the score was tied 2-2. The Soviet coach then made a controversial decision and replaced the person many believed to be the best goaltender in the world. That decision later led him to be second-guessed.

The second period started with the Soviets scoring an early goal to take a 3-2 lead. They pretty much dominated the second period; if it had not been for the superb play of goaltender Jim Craig, the Soviet lead heading into the third period would have been far greater than 3-2. The Soviets out-shot the Americans 12-2 in the second period.

The third period was intense. The U.S. was just 20 minutes away from a chance to play for the gold medal. The crowd was going crazy when Mark Johnson scored with around 11:30 left in the game to tie the score at 3-3. About one minute and twenty seconds later, Mike Eruzione gave the Americans the lead when he slapped a shot past the Soviet goaltender. The crowd erupted and remained standing and cheering for the last ten minutes. After a long and very exciting ten minutes that included many more incredible saves by Jim Craig, the miracle on ice came true. With about three seconds left, sports broadcaster Al Michaels asked the now-famous question: "Do you believe in miracles?" The answer was yes. The U.S. had won 4-3 and pulled off one of the greatest upsets and victories in sports history.

What many people forget was that, to win the gold medal, the U.S. had to come back and beat Finland. What was scary was that if the U.S. did not beat Finland, the team not only would not win the gold medal but might not win any medal at all. Herb Brooks understood that, so during the second intermission against Finland, with the U.S. trailing 2-1, Herb Brooks gave a short speech that was direct and to the point: "If you lose this game, you will take it to your *****ing graves." Then he turned to leave the locker room, stopped, turned back, and said, "Your *****ing graves." His players got the message. In the third period, the U.S. came out on a mission. The U.S. scored three unanswered goals and won the gold-medal game 4-2. The impossible dream had become a reality, and the fairytale story was complete. In my opinion, it is the greatest sports story of all time.

In 2002, I advanced to the finals of the men's singles table tennis tournament of the Kansas City Corporate Challenge. My road to the final that year was pretty smooth. I did have one defensive chopper that gave me some problems, but for the most part, it was clear sailing until the final.

The final matched me up with none other than Chunyen Liu of the company Garmin. Chunyen was ranked ninth in the state of Kansas at that time and was well respected around Kansas City as a top-notch table tennis player. He was from Taiwan, and being ranked ninth was probably a little underrated. In a tournament, Chunyen later beat the third-ranked player in Kansas and barely lost to Felix Xiao, formerly ranked first in Iowa. His match against Felix Xiao was probably the greatest table tennis match in Kansas City Corporate Challenge history. Chunyen eventually lost that close match in the fifth and final game. At the time, Chunyen also happened to work at Garmin, whose CEO was from Taiwan and was believed to like the sport of table tennis. It was rumored that Garmin had six Ping-Pong tables and held tournaments inside the company throughout the year. All rumors aside, however, I knew I had my hands full with Chunyen. I knew I was the underdog, too. Chunyen Liu was a better player than me but just like the 1980 Olympic hockey team, I believed in miracles. Remembering Herb Brook's speech, I thought, *If we played ten times, he might win nine, but not this match. Not tonight. Tonight I am the greatest table tennis player in the state.* I loved Herb Brooks. That guy was awesome.

I came out playing extremely well. Before Chunyen Liu could get settled into his game, I had won the first two games 11-9. I needed only one more game. One big advantage I had when I played Chunyen was that we had only faced each other a couple of times in practice prior to that. My style is a little unorthodox and tends to give people trouble when they're not used to it. I knew the match was far from over, though. Chunyen Liu was too good to roll over without a fight.

I wanted badly to knock him out in the third game but was unable to do it. Chunyen won game three 11-7. The momentum of the match had quickly shifted from me to him. The thing anyone learns when playing Chunyen Liu is that when he gets confident and starts smacking his forehand loops, his opponent is in deep trouble. Chunyen is an offensive player. I like to play defense, and I blocked loop shot after loop shot back, but in game four, I couldn't block enough back, and Chunyen won 11-8. It was now two games apiece. I knew I had to turn the momentum around if I was going to pull off the upset and win the gold medal.

Game five was tied at 5-5. I remember that by that time, everyone at the Overland Park Racquet Club was surrounding our table to watch. Quite a few people were there watching. I remember at this time of the match making a conscious decision to turn offensive and win or lose on my own terms. The next couple of points were two of the best points I ever remember playing. I blocked five or six of Chunyen's loops, and when I got the opportunity, I smashed two offensive winners past him. I ended up winning the fifth, decisive, game 11-8. That sticks in my mind as one of my greatest table tennis moments. To beat such a highly ranked player when it counted, with a title at stake and with a good number of people watching, was significant. Did it qualify as a miracle? A triple amputee beating the ninth-ranked player in Kansas in an Olympic sport? Yeah, in the world of sports, that was at least a small miracle.

In February 2010, Doug Hayden and I began meeting at the Gladstone Community Center pool to begin my training to swim the 50-yard freestyle in the

Kansas City Corporate Challenge. At the time, the last time I remembered swimming was twenty years earlier at the University of Kansas. I had taken swimming as an elective course and used swimming to cross-train for other sports. I remember having used to swim enough laps to equal a mile (72 lengths of the pool), but I had never been timed or competitive about swimming at all. Little did I know that Doug was about to give me a crash course in the lovely world of pain and suffering that only the fraternity of competitive swimmers truly understands. When you see those swimmers like Michael Phelps make winning their eight gold medals look easy on television, what you don't see is the years of swimming ten to twenty thousand yards per day in preparation. I knew swimming was a tough sport. Back in college, I had lived in the dorm with a guy who was on the Kansas University swimming team. He had also been an engineering student. His life had consisted of swimming for three hours twice per day, lifting weights, running, going to class, studying, and taking tests. Not an easy road. I had a huge respect for the guy.

It was late February 2010, so Doug and I had about four months to prepare for the Corporate Challenge swim meet that would begin June 21. I remember joking with Doug after I knew we had four months to prepare, saying, "Heck, I'll look like a supermodel by race day." Little did I know that it takes those big-time swimmers years of training to get those buffed bodies they show off to the world on national television. Not only had I not swum in twenty years, I hadn't done a sit-up in ten. I wasn't exactly sporting the six-pack great-swimmer look. I had mainly been playing table tennis for the past several years. Table tennis gets players in pretty good shape, but nothing like swimming does. Swimming conditions the whole body like few other sports can.

Prior to us meeting at the pool, Doug had been working on a one-arm swimming technique for me. He was really just hoping to find a way to get me down the pool and back and have me get a few breaths in without getting disqualified. Although Doug had competed as a diver at the University of Nebraska and had worked with and coached many different levels of swimmers, he had not worked with someone with the kind of disabilities I had. Honestly, neither one of us knew what to expect. It is interesting to note that world-class athlete and basketball player Shaquille O'Neal swam the 50-yard freestyle in 38.76 seconds when he took on Michael Phelps. Doug would later tell me that he was thinking from the beginning that breaking a minute in the 50-yard freestyle would be a great goal. He told me he had coached able-bodied swimmers for years who had never broken one minute.

Doug and I met at the Gladstone Community Center pool on a Saturday morning. I was pretty nervous. It had been so long since the last time I had swum, and I had never been timed before. One thing I did remember about swimming: If you're out of shape, don't try to be a hero the first time in the water. You will regret it. I took off my prosthetic legs and jumped in. Thankfully, I found out quickly that swimming is like riding a bike-you really never forget how. I indicated to Doug that I really only wanted to swim about 150 yards the first time back in the pool because I had made the mistake of going too far too fast before. The last time I had gone too far, I had barely been able to lift myself out of the pool. It was not a good feeling.

I think the main thing my new swimming coach wanted to get out of the first practice was to see how I swim and whether he was going to lose sleep at night trying to figure out what he had gotten himself into. We decided to start out by timing me in a 25-yard sprint down the pool. I was confident that I was in good enough shape to make it one length of the pool without Doug having to jump in and rescue me. Then again, twenty years is an awfully long time. Doug gave his version of "Swimmers on your mark! Beep!" I took off as fast as I could toward the other end of the pool. I couldn't remember how I was supposed to breathe, or anything. I think I was looking left and right and throwing my arm around as fast as I could. I hit the wall and quickly turned to Doug to see how I had done. To my amazement, I had swum my first 25 in twenty years in 24 seconds! I was really happy with that. My thinking was that whatever time I got, I could double it and have an idea of how fast I would eventually do the 50-yard once I was in shape. I then asked Doug to give me his honest analysis of my 25-yard scramble. Overall, he said he was amazed, but he was honest and realistic and said there were a lot of areas to improve. "It was a little chaotic. You were definitely competing. But overall, it's a great start." I went home that day extremely excited about the opportunity and adventure that lay ahead: a new sport, and one I might be pretty good at too.

Doug and I started meeting regularly at the pool every Wednesday evening and Saturday morning. In my second practice, I swam three hundred yards; in the third, I swam five hundred yards; and pretty soon, I was up to a thousand yards. I learned early on that two days a week weren't going to be anywhere near enough time in the pool to get me in the kind of shape I needed to be in so I joined the YMCA near where I lived and started swimming five days a week.

Doug Hayden is a great coach. I not only would never have started swimming but also would never have accomplished what lay ahead if it hadn't been for Doug. I had thought wrestling was the toughest sport out there after I had wrestled in high school and a little in college, but after Doug introduced me to competitive swimming, I had to rethink my toughest-sport theory. Swimming can be outright brutal. What swimmers have to put their bodies through to shave hundredths of a second off their times is crazy.

One of the hardest things about swimming is the breathing. If one could somehow wear an oxygen mask, swimming would be fairly easy. It's balancing the need to go fast with the body's need for oxygen that makes swimming a lot more complicated than it looks on television. When I first started swimming, I was breathing way too much. I was turning my head to the left and right to breathe. Anywhere I could get a breath, I wanted one. That's where having a good coach comes in handy. A good coach will tell an athlete what he or she is doing wrong and can lift the athlete's spirits when he or she feels like quitting. Doug is very good at encouraging me when I'm down. He also has a great sense of humor. In one of the first practices we had, I had come up choking on a lot of water. He had commented something like, "Yeah, you're not suppose to breathe while you're underwater." I had thought, *That's just great, I've got a smart aleck for a coach!* Doug does an excellent job, though, of pushing me, encouraging me, and keeping the mood light by making me laugh. Swimmers need all three when they're training, because swimming is hard work.

Three months into the training, I still had not broken 50 seconds for 50 yards. I was a little discouraged. I had thought when I timed a 24-second 25-yard my first time in the pool that would all but guarantee that I could do 50 yards in under 50 seconds. My first 25 yards had dropped to 23 seconds. The problem was that my second 25 yards were coming in around 27.5 seconds. Then one day in practice, Doug was able to get me to understand that it's all about traction in the water. Amateur swimmers like myself have a tendency to believe that swimming fast is all about the number of strokes they do. But it's not. Swimming fast is all about long, effective strokes, not the number of strokes. I didn't realize it, but what I had been doing by trying to go fast was simply spinning my wheels. So how did Doug get me to see it? He timed me when I wasn't expecting him to. He waited for me to take off swimming down a length of the pool when I was just relaxed and casual as could be. When I got to the end of the pool, he asked, "Do you know how fast you were?"

"No. How fast?" I asked.

"Twenty point nine seconds" Doug responded with a grin on his face. I could not believe it. That day, we turned the corner on our swimming journey. After that, it was not a question of whether we would break 50 seconds, but of how much we would break it by.

The last month prior to the Corporate Challenge swim meet, Doug had me start doing what swimmers call tapering off. Instead of swimming about 1,200 yards five days a week, I cut it down to 500 or 600 yards. I also started doing a lot more 25-yard sprints. I guess the whole idea of tapering off is to give your muscles time to rebuild and recover. We had spent three months tearing my muscles down. I didn't mind tapering down. A little less work sounded good to me. Even in this tapering-down period, though, my times kept dropping. At least once per practice, I would time myself in the 50. By the time race week came, I was regularly clocking in times just below 50 seconds. My fastest practice race was 48 seconds.

I was really nervous during the week leading up to the race. Two weeks earlier, my partner and I had beaten Sprint to win the gold medal in doubles table tennis for the Corporate Challenge. I had thought I would relax after that and just enjoy my newfound sport. I was wrong. All I could think about up to my big swim day were all the little things that could go wrong. I could false start. I could put my goggles on wrong so they would leak. When I took my first breath, I might take in a mouthful of water and choke. I might not breathe enough in the first 25 yards and become hypoxic. If that happened I could forget a good time. At that point, all a swimmer cares about is getting as much oxygen into the body as quickly as possible. I could mis-time reaching the wall and have a slow turn. I could never gain traction in the water and just spin my wheels. It was amazing. The more I learned about swimming, the more I worried about all the things that could go wrong so I finally decided that the smart thing to do was to just turn the swim and all my fears over to God. I just told God that I couldn't do it on my own and needed Him to carry me. I promised God that if He helped me swim fast, I would give Him all the glory!

Swim day arrived: June 23, 2010, a day that Doug and I will never forget. I think I probably drove Doug nuts leading up to the big swim. He could sense my anxiety. He admitted that even though he was an experienced veteran swimmer, he still got nervous on race day. There is a lot of uncertainty in swimming, as with all sports. No matter how much you prepare you never know for sure what's going to happen. It's why Chris Berman says on ESPN during football season, "That's why they play the games."

I was scheduled to swim around 6:50 p.m. I got to the pool around 6:00 p.m. and was having one of my minor shaking attacks. I have hypoglycemia, which means at times, my blood sugar level gets too low. It's usually an easy problem to solve as long as I have access to some food or drink with sugar in it. Of course I had forgotten to bring any money, so my swimming teammate saved my day by lending me money to buy a Snickers bar and a big bottle of Gatorade. Little did I know that my low sugar attack might have been a blessing in disguise. In any case, something gave me an extra boost of energy that had escaped me in my prior swims. Doug and the other swimming team coordinator, Christine Franz, had checked me in and arranged with officials to get me specially placed into lane 1 and heat 1. This allowed me to take my legs off next to the pool and scoot just a few feet into lane 1 when my heat time was up.

I was all set. My heat time was about five minutes away. I tried in my mind to simplify my race as much as I could. I told myself to just get down to the first wall in 22 or 23 seconds and give myself a chance to bring it home. I wasn't even thinking of the second 25 yards. I told myself to just get in a position where I could gut it out in the last half. Doug had told me that adrenaline would take over in front of the big crowd. As it turned out, maybe it was adrenaline and a few thousand grams of sugar. Whatever it was, it worked. I can hear the words again like they were yesterday: "Swimmers, on your mark!" Beep! I could not have timed my start any better. I took off at a very high pace and was able to get good traction in the water right away. I took my first breath about halfway down the first length of the pool. I know I had set a very fast pace, because I became a little hypoxic and took two quick breaths around the flags. I then took my fourth breath when I hit the wall to turn. Even though that was one more breath than I usually took, it really set me up for my best finish ever. I hit the first wall in 22 seconds. Usually in the second 25, I was lucky if I could make it back in less than 27 seconds. This day was different, though. This day would turn out looking like a day on which God intervened on my behalf. The more I look back at all the circumstances that lined up in my favor, the more I believe that God clearly answered my prayer and helped me swim fast. I honestly don't even remember swimming the last 25. I've watched it on tape a few thousand times: 45.25 seconds! (See the YouTube video "Triple Amputee Swims.") My time was better than that of 130 able-bodied swimmers in the 50-yard freestyle of the Kansas City Corporate Challenge. Only 6.5 seconds behind Shaq! Do I believe in miracles? Oh yeah!

Why is it so hard for us to believe in miracles? To me, the fact that I even exist is a miracle. Where was I one hundred years ago? Life is miraculous. I heard we have more than 100,000 miles of blood vessels in our bodies and they transport blood throughout our bodies every 29 seconds! If you stretched out your blood vessels, they would wrap around the world three times! Take our sun for example. The sun is by far the largest object in the solar system. It just happens to be a perfect distance from the earth to keep us warm. Any further away, and we would all freeze to death. Any closer, and we would all burn up. God is awesome!

Why do we have such a hard time believing in miracles? When I read my Bible, I see that Jesus was less frustrated with people's sins than with their unbelief. Time and time again, Jesus said that with God, all things are possible. Jesus basically said that if we just believe, anything is possible.

I believe in the God of all miracles. I believe in a God who pulls off the impossible on a daily basis. But the best part about God is that He not only is a God of miracles but is a giver. God has given me everything. He gave me my very life. He gave me my parents. He has given me all of my talents. He gives me my next breath. The Bible says that He gave us His only Son to die on the cross for our sins. John 3:16 says, "For God so loved the world that He gave His one and only Son, that whoever believes in Him shall not perish but have eternal life." A selfless God like that is a God worth living for. Whenever I compete in sports, I compete for His glory! I win for His glory! I wrote this book for His glory, and I will worship Him forever! Do I believe in miracles? Yes!

CPSIA information can be obtained
at www.ICGtesting.com
Printed in the USA
FFOW02n2104060315
11628FF